The Constitution of the
State of Arkansas
A Quick Reference Guide

Bootblack Budget Books
Copyright 2018 ©
ISBN-13: 978-1985665101
ISBN-10: 1985665107

Preamble – Page 30

Article I: Boundaries and
Seat of Government – Page 31

Section 1. Boundaries

Section 2. Seat of Government

Article II: Declaration of Rights – Page 32

Section 1. Authority of government

Section 2. Individual liberty

Section 3. Legal equality

Section 4. Freedom of assembly; petition

Section 5. Freedom to bear arms

Section 6. Freedom of speech; press; criminal prosecutions for libel

Section 7. Jury trials; rights

Section 8. Criminal procedure; double jeopardy; right against self-incrimination; due process

Section 9. Bail; limitations on penalties; detention of witnesses

Section 10. Rights of defendant

Section 11. Habeas corpus

Section 12. Abrogation of laws prohibited

Section 13. Remedies
Section 14. Treason

Section 15. Searches and seizures

Section 16. Incarceration for debt prohibited

Section 17. Attainder; ex post facto laws; impairment of contract

Section 18. Privileges and immunities; nondiscrimination

Section 19. Perpetuities and monopolies prohibited

Section 20. Resident aliens and citizens; property rights

Section 21. Fundamental rights of life, liberty, property; exile prohibited

Section 22. Compensation for property

Section 23. Taxation and eminent domain; delegation

Section 24. Freedom of religion

Section 25. Religious freedom protected

Section 26. Religious discrimination prohibited

Section 27. Slavery prohibited; military authority limited

Section 28. Feudal land tenures prohibited

Section 29. Additional rights not precluded

Article III: Franchise and Elections – Page 38

Section 1. Qualifications of electors

Section 2. Right of suffrage

Section 4. Arrest; immunity while voting

Section 6. Election laws; violations

Section 7. Military personnel; voting

Section 8. Time of holding elections

Section 9. Contested elections; witness testimony

Section 10. Election officers

Section 11. Tallying votes

Section 12. Proxies; viva voce voting

Section 13. Procedures for elections with one candidate

Article IV: Departments – Page 40

Section 1. Division of governmental authority

Section 2. Separation of powers

Article V: Legislative Department – Page 41

Section 1. General Assembly--Initiative and Referendum

Section 2. House of Representatives

Section 3. Senate

Section 4. General Assembly members; requirements

Section 5. Regular and fiscal sessions

Section 6. General Assembly vacancies

Section 7. Government officers; eligibility

Section 8. Public funds; eligibility of collector or holder

Section 9. Persons convicted ineligible

Section 10. Assembly members; ineligible to hold civil office

Section 11. Selection of officers; quorum

Section 12. Authority and obligations

Section 13. Open sessions; exception

Section 14. Appointment of officers; ratification

Section 15. Privilege from arrest of members; freedom of speech or debate

Section 17. Duration of sessions

Section 18. Election of presiding officers

Section 19. Laws; enacting language

Section 20. Sovereign immunity of the State of Arkansas

Section 21. Bills and amendments

Section 22. Bills; passage by vote

Section 23. Prohibition against revival, amendment, or extension of laws

Section 24. Local and special matters; legislation prohibited

Section 25. Special legislation; prohibition

Section 26. Local and special legislation; notice and publication

Section 27. Additional compensation; legislative appropriations

Section 28. Adjournments; limitations

Section 29. Appropriations

Section 30. General and special appropriations

Section 31. Appropriations and taxes; use

Section 32. Workers' Compensation

Section 33. Corporate obligations to State

Section 34. Introduction of bills--Time limit

Section 35. Bribery; felony

Section 36. Criminal indictment; expulsion

Section 37. Laws; enactment by majority

Section 38. Tax increases; approval=

Section 39. State expenses--Limitation--Exceptions

Section 40. General appropriation bill--Enactment

Section 41. Obligations incurred by legislation

Section 42. Review and approval of administrative rules

Article VI: Executive Department – Page 56

Section 1. Executive department officers

Section 2. Governor

Section 3. Executive officers; elections

Section 4. Contested elections; executive officers

Section 5. Governor; requirements

Section 6. Governor; military commander-in-chief

Section 7. Governor; reporting requirements

Section 8. Governor; address to General Assembly

Section 9. State Seal

Section 10. Grants and commissions; issuance

Section 11. Governor's office exclusive

Section 12. President of Senate; gubernatorial succession

Section 13. Speaker of House; gubernatorial succession

Section 14. Governor; vacancy

Section 15. Legislation; approval or veto

Section 16. Concurrent resolutions or orders; endorsement or veto

Section 17. Line item veto

Section 18. Executive clemency

Section 19. Special sessions of Assembly

Section 20. General Assembly; adjournment by Governor

Section 21. Secretary of State; duties

Section 22. Executive officers; duties

Section 23. Governor; commissions

Article VII: Judicial Department – Page 63

Section 19. Circuit clerks--Election--Term of office--Ex officio duties--County clerks elected in certain counties

Section 23. Jury instructions

Section 26. Indirect contempt

Section 27. Impeachment of local officials

Section 28. County Courts; jurisdiction

Section 29. County judge--Election--Term--Qualifications

Section 30. County justices of peace

Section 31. Terms of county courts

Section 33. Judgments of courts; appeals

Section 36. Commission of special judges

Section 37. County judge; compensation, powers

Section 38. Election; justices of peace

Section 41. Justice of peace; residence

Section 46. County executive officers--Compensation of county assessor

Section 47. Election of constable

Section 48. Officers; commissioned by Governor

Section 49. Writs and process; indictments

Section 51. City, etc. allowances; appeals

Section 52. Election contests; appeals

Section 53. County officers ineligible to civil office

Article VIII: Apportionment--Membership in General Assembly – Page 69

Section 1. Board of Apportionment

Section 2. House of Representatives; members

Section 3. Senate; members, districts

Section 4. Reapportionment by board; report

Section 5. State Supreme Court; jurisdiction

Section 6. Elections following apportionment

Article IX: Exemption – Page 71

Section 1. Exemptions of personal property; unmarried residents; residents not heads of households

Section 2. Exemptions of personal property; married residents; heads of families

Section 3. Homestead exemption

Section 4. Homestead outside city, etc.

Section 5. Homestead in city, etc.

Section 6. Widows; children; entitlement in homestead

Section 7. Property of married woman

Section 8. Married women; scheduling personal property

Section 9. Application of exemptions; 1868 Constitution

Section 10. Minor children; homestead benefits

Article X: Agriculture, Mining and Manufacture – Page 74

Section 1. Creation of mining, manufacturing and agricultural bureau

Section 2. Office of State Geologist

Section 3. Capital investments; taxation exemption

Article XI: Militia – Page 75

Section 1. Composition of militia

Section 2. Formation of volunteer companies

Section 3. Privileges from arrest

Section 4. Governor's power to call

Article XII: Municipal and Private Corporations – Page 76

Section 1. Invalidity of charters, grants

Section 2. Special acts; passage prohibited

Section 3. Organization; cities and towns

Section 4. Fiscal affairs; bond issuance

Section 5. Political subdivisions not to become stockholders in or lend credit to private corporations--Exceptions

Section 6. Formation of corporations; laws

Section 7. State prohibited from stockholding

Section 8. Private corporations; stock issuance

Section 9. Property; appropriation to use of corporation

Section 10. Bills, notes, etc.; issuance

Section 11. Foreign corporation doing business in this state; rules

Section 12. Prohibition of state's assumption of liabilities

Article XIII: Counties, County Seats and County Lines – Page 80

Section 1. Counties; area

Section 2. Altering county lines; consent of voters

Section 3. County seat changes; consent of voters

Section 4. New county lines

Section 5. Districts within Sebastian County

Article XIV: Education – Page 81

Section 1. Free public schools

Section 2. Public school fund; use

Section 3. School districts--Tax levies

Section 4. Public school supervision

Article XV: Impeachment and Address – Page 84

Section 1. Officials subject to impeachment; conditions

Section 2. Impeachment powers of the House; trial by the Senate

Section 3. Removal of officers; Governor

Article XVI: Finance and Taxation – Page 85

Section 1. Prohibition of lending of credit by government entities

Section 2. Payment of State debts

Section 3. Unauthorized profit-making

Section 4. Salaries and fees of state officers

Section 5. Property; taxation by value; exemptions

Section 6. Additional tax exemption laws void

Section 7. Taxation of corporations; power

Section 8. Levying State taxes; rate

Section 9. Levying of county taxes

Section 10. County, etc. taxes; payment

Section 11. Tax levies; requirements

Section 12. Disbursement of funds--Appropriation required

Section 13. Protection against enforcement of illegal exactions

Section 14. Property reappraisals; tax adjustments

Section 15. Residential property and other types of land; assessment according to usage

Section 16. Residence exemption; age 65

Article XVII: Railroads, Canals and Turnpikes – Page 93

Section 1. Railroad construction rights; common carriers

Section 2. Maintenance of offices within the state

Section 3. Equal rights of transportation

Section 4. Property, stock consolidation prohibited

Section 5. Officers; personal interest prohibited

Section 6. Prohibition of carrier discrimination

Section 7. Prohibition of free passes

Section 8. Forfeiture of charters; remission

Section 9. Eminent domain

Section 10. Law enforcement; carrier regulations

Section 11. Movable property; execution, sale

Section 12. Responsibility for damages

Section 13. Reports

Article XVIII: Judicial Circuits – Page 97

Section 1. Composition of judicial circuits

Article XIX: Miscellaneous Provisions – Page 102

Section 1. Disqualification of atheists

Section 2. Dueling; disqualification

Section 3. Officeholders required to possess qualifications of electors

Section 4. Civil officers; residence requirements

Section 5. Officers; continuation following expiration of term

Section 6. Holding multiple offices prohibited

Section 7. Absences not affecting residency

Section 8. Salary deductions for neglect of duty

Section 9. Permanent offices; creation limited

Section 10. Secretary of State; election returns

Section 12. Receipts and expenditures; publication

Section 14. Lotteries

Section 16. Contract awards; buildings, bridges

Section 17. State laws; revisions, publication, etc.

Section 18. Securing safety; mining employees travelers on railroads, public conveyances

Section 19. Certain disabled persons; support

Section 20. Oath of office of public officeholders

Section 21. Sureties upon official bonds

Section 22. Amendments to the Constitution

Section 24. Mode of contesting elections

Section 25. State seal

Section 26. Officers filling of offices

Section 27. Assessments for local improvements

Section 28. Contributions

Section 29. Registration as a lobbyist by a former member of the General Assembly

Section 30. Gifts from lobbyists

Section 31. Independent citizens commission

Article XX: "Holford" Bonds Not to Be Paid – Page 122

Section 1. "Holford" bonds not to be paid

Schedule – Page 123

Section 1. Continuation of current laws

Section 3. Elections

Section 4. Voter qualification

Section 5. Election notice

Section 6. Proclamation issuance by Governor

Section 7. Election supervisors; State board

Section 8. Election supervisors; county board

Section 9. Poll-books; form

Section 10. Distribution of Constitution copies

Section 11. Appointment of election judges, clerks

Section 12. Means of conducting elections

Section 13. Words on ballot ticket

Section 14. Voting procedure

Section 15. Dram shops, etc.; closure

Section 16. Opening, closing of polls

Section 17. Results; counting and publication

Section 18. Commissioning of officers; Governor

Section 19. Representatives and Senators; election

Section 20. Assumption of officer duties

Section 21. Incumbents; vacation of office

Section 22. Commencement of first session

Section 23. Courts regarded as continuations

Section 24. Continuation of incumbents; conditions

Section 25. Fraudulent behavior during election

Section 26. Time of holding offices

Section 27. Election expenses; appropriations

Section 28. Compensation and salaries

PREAMBLE

We, the People of the State of Arkansas, grateful to Almighty God for the privilege of choosing our own form of government; for our civil and religious liberty; and desiring to perpetuate its blessings, and secure the same to our selves and posterity; do ordain and establish this Constitution.

Article I: Boundaries and Seat of Government

Section 1. Boundaries
We do declare and establish, ratify and confirm, the following as the permanent boundaries of the State of Arkansas, that is to say: Beginning at the middle of the main channel of the Mississippi River, on the parallel of thirty-six degrees of north latitude, running thence west with said parallel of latitude to the middle of the main channel of the St. Francis River; thence up the main channel of said last-named river to the parallel of thirty-six degrees thirty minutes of north latitude; thence west with the southern boundary line of the State of Missouri to the southwest corner of said last-named state; thence to be bounded on the west to the north bank of Red River, as by act of Congress and treaties existing January 1, 1837, defining the western limits of the Territory of Arkansas, and to be bounded across and south of Red River by the boundary line of the State of Texas as far as to the northwest corner of the State of Louisiana; thence easterly with the northern boundary line of said last-named State to the middle of the main channel of the Mississippi River; thence up the middle of the main channel of said last-named river, including an island in said river known as "Belle Point Island," and all other land originally surveyed and included as a part of the Territory or State of Arkansas, to the thirty-sixth degree of north latitude, the place of beginning.

Section 2. Seat of Government
The seat of government of the state of Arkansas shall be and remain at Little Rock, where it is now established.

Article II: Declaration of Rights

Section 1. Source of power.
All political power is inherent in the people and government is instituted for their protection, security and benefit; and they have the right to alter, reform or abolish the same, in such manner as they may think proper.

Section 2. Freedom and independence.
All men are created equally free and independent, and have certain inherent and inalienable rights; amongst which are those of enjoying and defending life and liberty; of acquiring, possessing and protecting property, and reputation; and of pursuing their own happiness. To secure these rights governments are instituted among men, deriving their just powers from the consent of the governed.

Section 3. Equality before the law.
The equality of all persons before the law is recognized, and shall ever remain inviolate; nor shall any citizen ever be deprived of any right, privilege or immunity; nor exempted from any burden or duty, on account of race, color or previous condition.

Section 4. Right of assembly and of petition.
The right of the people peaceably to assemble, to consult for the common good; and to petition, by address or remonstrance, the government, or any department thereof, shall never be abridged.

Section 5. Right to bear arms.
The citizens of this State shall have the right to keep and bear arms, for their common defense.

Section 6. Liberty of the press and of speech — Libel.
The liberty of the press shall forever remain inviolate. The free communication of thoughts and opinions, is one of the invaluable rights of man; and all persons may freely write and publish their sentiments on all subjects, being responsible for the abuse of such right. In all criminal prosecutions for libel, the truth may be

given in evidence to the jury; and, if it shall appear to the jury that the matter charged as libelous is true, and was published with good motives and for justifiable ends, the party charged shall be acquitted.

Section 7. Jury trial — Right to — Waiver — Civil cases — Nine jurors agreeing.
The right of trial by jury shall remain inviolate, and shall extend to all cases at law, without regard to the amount in controversy; but a jury trial may be waived by the parties in all cases in the manner prescribed by law; and in all jury trials in civil cases, where as many as nine of the jurors agree upon a verdict, the verdict so agreed upon shall be returned as the verdict of such jury, provided, however, that where a verdict is returned by less than twelve jurors all the jurors consenting to such verdict shall sign the same.

Section 8. Criminal charges — Self-incrimination — Due process — Double jeopardy — Bail.
No person shall be held to answer a criminal charge unless on the presentment or indictment of a grand jury, except in cases of impeachment or cases such as the General Assembly shall make cognizable by justices of the peace, and courts of similar jurisdiction; or cases arising in the army and navy of the United States; or in the militia, when in actual service in time of war or public danger; and no person, for the same offense, shall be twice put in jeopardy of life or liberty; but if, in any criminal prosecution, the jury be divided in opinion, the court before which the trial shall be had, may, in its discretion, discharge the jury, and commit or bail the accused for trial, at the same or the next term of said court; nor shall any person be compelled, in any criminal case, to be a witness against himself; nor be deprived of life, liberty or property, without due process of law. All persons shall, before conviction, be bailable by sufficient sureties, except for capital offenses, when the proof is evident or the presumption great.

Section 9. Excessive bail or punishment prohibited — Witnesses — Detention.
Excessive bail shall not be required; nor shall excessive fines be imposed; nor shall cruel or unusual punishments be inflicted; nor witnesses be unreasonably detained.

Section 10. Right of accused enumerated — Change of venue.
In all criminal prosecutions, the accused shall enjoy the right to a speedy and public trial by an impartial jury of the county in which the crime shall have been committed; provided, that the venue may be changed to any other county of the judicial district in which the indictment is found, upon the application of the accused, in such manner as now is, or may be prescribed by law; and to be informed of the nature and cause of the accusation against him, and to have a copy thereof; and to be confronted with the witnesses against him; to have compulsory process for obtaining witnesses in his favor, and to be heard by himself and his counsel.

Section 11. Habeas corpus.
The privilege of the writ of habeas corpus shall not be suspended; except by the General Assembly, in case of rebellion, insurrection or invasion, when the public safety may require it.

Section 12. Suspension of laws.
No power of suspending or setting aside the law or laws of the State, shall ever be exercised, except by the General Assembly.

Section 13. Redress of wrongs.
Every person is entitled to a certain remedy in the laws for all injuries or wrongs he may receive in his person, property or character; he ought to obtain justice freely, and without purchase; completely, and without denial; promptly and without delay; conformably to the laws.

Section 14. Treason.
Treason against the State shall only consist in levying and making war against the same, or in adhering to its enemies, giving them aid and comfort. No person shall be convicted of treason unless on the testimony of two witnesses to the same overt act, or on confession in open court.

Section 15. Unreasonable searches and seizures.
The right of the people of this State to be secure in their persons, houses, papers, and effects, against unreasonable searches and seizures, shall not be violated; and no warrant shall issue, except upon probable cause, supported by oath or affirmation, and particularly describing the place to be searched, and the person or thing to be seized.

Section 16. Imprisonment for debt.
No person shall be imprisoned for debt in any civil action, on mesne or final process, unless in cases of fraud.

Section 17. Attainder — Ex post facto laws.
 No bill of attainder, ex post facto law, or law impairing the obligation of contracts shall ever be passed; and no conviction shall work corruption of blood or forfeiture of estate.

Section 18. Privileges and immunities — Equality.
The General Assembly shall not grant to any citizen, or class of citizens, privileges or immunities which, upon the same terms, shall not equally belong to all citizens.

Section 19. Perpetuities and monopolies.
Perpetuities and monopolies are contrary to the genius of a republic, and shall not be allowed; nor shall any hereditary emoluments, privileges or honors ever be granted or conferred in this State.

Section 20. Resident aliens — Descent of property.
No distinction shall ever be made by law, between resident aliens and citizens, in regard to the possession, enjoyment or descent of property.

Section 21. Life, liberty and property — Banishment prohibited.
No person shall be taken, or imprisoned, or disseized of his estate, freehold, liberties or privileges; or outlawed, or in any manner destroyed, or deprived of his life, liberty or property; except by the judgment of his peers, or the law of the land; nor shall any person, under any circumstances, be exiled from the State.

Section 22. Property rights — Taking without just compensation prohibited.
The right of property is before and higher than any constitutional sanction; and private property shall not be taken, appropriated or damaged for public use, without just compensation therefor.

Section 23. Eminent domain and taxation.
The State's ancient right of eminent domain and of taxation, is herein fully and expressly conceded; and the General Assembly may delegate the taxing power, with the necessary restriction, to the State's subordinate political and municipal corporations, to the extent of providing for their existence, maintenance and well being, but no further.

Section 24. Religious liberty.
All men have a natural and indefeasible right to worship Almighty God according to the dictates of their own consciences; no man can, of right, be compelled to attend, erect, or support any place of worship; or to maintain any ministry against his consent. No human authority can, in any case or manner whatsoever, control or interfere with the right of conscience; and no preference shall ever be given, by law, to any religious establishment, denomination or mode of worship, above any other.

Section 25. Protection of religion.
Religion, morality and knowledge being essential to good government, the General Assembly shall enact suitable laws to protect every religious denomination in the peaceable enjoyment of its own mode of public worship.

Section 26. Religious tests.
No religious test shall ever be required of any person as a qualification to vote or hold office; nor shall any person be rendered incompetent to be a witness on account of his religious belief; but nothing herein shall be construed to dispense with oaths or affirmations.

Section 27. Slavery — Standing armies — Military subordinate to civil power.
There shall be no slavery in this State, nor involuntary servitude, except as a punishment for crime. No standing army shall be kept in time of peace; the military shall, at all times, be in strict subordination to the civil power; and no soldier shall be quartered in any house, or on any premises, without the consent of the owner, in time of peace; nor in time of war, except in a manner prescribed by law.

Section 28. Tenure of lands.
All lands in this State are declared to be allodial; and feudal tenures of every description, with all their incidents, are prohibited.

Section 29. Enumeration of rights of people not exclusive of other rights — Protection against encroachment.
This enumeration of rights shall not be construed to deny or disparage others retained by the people; and to guard against any encroachments on the rights herein retained, or any transgression of any of the higher powers herein delegated, we declare that everything in this article is excepted out of the general powers of the government; and shall forever remain inviolate; and that all laws contrary thereto, or to the other provisions herein contained, shall be void.

Article III: Franchise and Elections

Section 1. Qualifications of electors.
Except as otherwise provided by this Constitution, any person may vote in an election in this state who is:

(1) A citizen of the United States;
(2) A resident of the State of Arkansas;
(3) At least eighteen (18) years of age; and
(4) Lawfully registered to vote in the election.

Section 2. Right of suffrage.
Elections shall be free and equal. No power, civil or military, shall ever interfere to prevent the free exercise of the right of suffrage; nor shall any law be enacted whereby such right shall be impaired or forfeited, except for the commission of a felony, upon lawful conviction thereof.

Section 3.

Repealed.

Section 4. Privilege of electors from arrest.
Electors shall, in all cases (except treason, felony and breach of the peace,) be privileged from arrest during their attendance at elections, and going to and from the same.

Section 5.

Repealed.

Section 6. Violation of election laws — Penalty.
Any persons who shall be convicted of fraud, bribery, or other willful and corrupt violation of any election law of this State, shall be adjudged guilty of a felony, and disqualified from holding any office of trust or profit in this State.

Section 7. Soldiers and sailors — Residence — Voting rights.
No soldier, sailor, or marine, in the military or naval service of the United States, shall acquire a residence by reason of being stationed on duty in this State.

Section 8. Time of holding elections.
The general elections shall be held biennially, on the days and at times fixed by the General Assembly.

Section 9. Testimony in election contest — Self-incrimination.
In trials of contested elections and in proceedings for the investigation of elections, no person shall be permitted to withhold his testimony on the ground that it may incriminate himself or subject him to public infamy: but such testimony shall not be used against him in any judicial proceeding, except for perjury in giving such testimony.

Section 10. Election officers.
The General Assembly shall determine the qualifications of an election officer.

Section 11. Votes to be counted.
If the officers of any election shall unlawfully refuse or fail to receive, count, or return the vote or ballot of any qualified elector, such vote or ballot shall nevertheless be counted upon the trial of any contests arising out of said election.

Section 12. Elections by representative — Viva voce vote.
All elections by persons acting in a representative capacity shall be viva voce.

Article IV: Departments

Section 1. Departments of government.
The powers of the government of the State of Arkansas shall be divided into three distinct departments, each of them to be confided to a separate body of magistracy, to-wit: Those which are legislative, to one, those which are executive, to another, and those which are judicial, to another.

Section 2. Separation of departments.
No person or collection of persons, being of one of these departments, shall exercise any power belonging to either of the others, except in the instances hereinafter expressly directed or permitted.

Article V: Legislative Department

Section 1. Initiative and Referendum.
The legislative power of the people of this State shall be vested in a General Assembly, which shall consist of the Senate and House of Representatives, but the people reserve to themselves the power to propose legislative measures, laws and amendments to the Constitution, and to enact or reject the same at the polls independent of the General Assembly; and also reserve the power, at their own option to approve or reject at the polls any entire act or any item of an appropriation bill.
Initiative. The first power reserved by the people is the initiative. Eight per cent of the legal voters may propose any law and ten per cent may propose a constitutional amendment by initiative petition and every such petition shall include the full text of the measure so proposed. Initiative petitions for state-wide measures shall be filed with the Secretary of State not less than four months before the election at which they are to be voted upon; provided, that at least thirty days before the aforementioned filing, the proposed measure shall have been published once, at the expense of the petitioners, in some paper of general circulation. Referendum. The second power reserved by the people is the referendum, and any number not less than six per cent of the legal voters may, by petition, order the referendum against any general Act, or any item of an appropriation bill, or measure passed by the General Assembly, but the filing of a referendum petition against one or more items, sections or parts of any such act or measure shall not delay the remainder from becoming operative. Such petition shall be filed with the Secretary of State not later than ninety days after the final adjournment of the session at which such Act was passed, except when a recess or adjournment shall be taken temporarily for a longer period than ninety days, in which case such petition shall be filed not later than ninety days after such recess or temporary adjournment. Any measure referred to the people by referendum petition shall remain in abeyance until such vote is taken. The total number of votes cast for the office of Governor

in the last preceding general election shall be the basis upon which the number of signatures of legal voters upon state-wide initiative and referendum petitions shall be computed.

Upon all initiative or referendum petitions provided for in any of the sections of this article, it shall be necessary to file from at least fifteen of the counties of the State, petitions bearing the signature of not less than one-half of the designated percentage of the electors of such county. Emergency. If it shall be necessary for the preservation of the public peace, health and safety that a measure shall become effective without delay, such necessity shall be stated in one section, and if upon a yea and nay vote two-thirds of all the members elected to each house, or two-thirds of all the members elected to city or town councils, shall vote upon separate roll call in favor of the measure going into immediate operation, such emergency measure shall become effective without delay. It shall be necessary, however, to state the fact which constitutes such emergency. Provided, however, that an emergency shall not be declared on any franchise or special privilege or act creating any vested right or interest or alienating any property of the State. If a referendum is filed against any emergency measure such measure shall be a law until it is voted upon by the people, and if it is then rejected by a majority of the electors voting thereon, it shall be thereby repealed. The provision of this sub-section shall apply to city or town councils. Local for Municipalities and Counties. The initiative and referendum powers of the people are hereby further reserved to the legal voters of each municipality and county as to all local, special and municipal legislation of every character in and for their respective municipalities and counties, but no local legislation shall be enacted contrary to the Constitution or any general law of the State, and any general law shall have the effect of repealing any local legislation which is in conflict therewith. Municipalities may provide for the exercise of the initiative and referendum as to their local legislation. General laws shall be enacted providing for the exercise of the initiative and referendum as to counties. Fifteen per cent of the legal voters of any municipality or county may order the referendum, or invoke the initiative upon any local measure. In municipalities the number of signatures required upon any petition shall be computed upon the total vote cast for the office of mayor at the last preceding general election; in counties upon the office of circuit clerk. In municipalities and counties the time for filing an initiative petition shall not be fixed at less than sixty days nor more than ninety days before the election at which it is to be voted upon; for a referendum petition at not less than thirty days nor more than ninety days after the passage of such measure by a municipal council; nor less than ninety days when filed against a local or special measure passed by the General Assembly. Every extension, enlargement, grant, or conveyance of a franchise or any rights, property, easement, lease, or occupation of or in any road, street, alley or any part thereof in real property or interest in real property owned by municipalities, exceeding in value three hundred dollars, whether the same be by statute, ordinance, resolution, or otherwise, shall be subject to referendum and shall not be subject to emergency legislation.

General Provisions

Definition. The word "measure" as used herein includes any bill, law, resolution, ordinance, charter, constitutional amendment or legislative proposal or enactment of any character. No Veto. The veto power of the Governor or mayor shall not extend to measures initiated by or referred to the people. Amendment and Repeal. No measure approved by a vote of the people shall be amended or repealed by the General Assembly or by any city council, except upon a yea and nay vote on roll call of two-thirds of all the members elected to each house of the General Assembly, or of the city council, as the case may be. Election. All measures initiated by the people whether for the State, county, city or town, shall be submitted only at the regular elections, either State, congressional or municipal, but referendum petitions may be referred to the people at special elections to be called by the proper official, and such special elections shall be called when fifteen per cent of the legal voters shall petition for such special election, and if the referendum is invoked as to any measure passed by a city or town council, such city or town council may order a special election. Majority. Any measure submitted to the people as herein provided shall take effect and become a law when approved by a majority of the votes cast upon such measure, and not otherwise, and shall not be required to receive a majority of the electors voting at such election. Such measures shall be operative on and after the thirtieth day after the election at which it is approved, unless otherwise specified in the Act. This section shall not be construed to deprive any member of the General Assembly of the right to introduce any measure, but no measure shall be submitted to the people by the General Assembly, except a proposed constitutional amendment or amendments as provided for in this Constitution. Canvass and Declaration of Results. The result of the vote upon any State measure shall be canvassed and declared by the State Board of Election Commissioners (or legal substitute therefor); upon a municipal or county measure, by the county election commissioners (or legal substitute therefor). Conflicting Measures. If conflicting measures initiated or referred to the people shall be approved by a majority of the votes severally cast for and against the same at the same election, the one receiving the highest number of affirmative votes shall become law.

The Petition

Title.
At the time of filing petitions the exact title to be used on the ballot shall by the petitioners be submitted with the petition, and on state-wide measures, shall be submitted to the State Board of Election Commissioners, who shall certify such title to the Secretary of State, to be placed upon the ballot; on county and municipal measures such title shall be submitted to the county election board and shall by said board be placed upon the ballot in such county or municipal election. Limitation. No limitation shall be placed upon the number of constitutional amendments, laws, or other measures which may be proposed and submitted to the people by either initiative or referendum petition as provided in this section. No petition shall be held invalid if it shall

contain a greater number of signatures than required herein. Verification. Only legal votes shall be counted upon petitions. Petitions may be circulated and presented in parts, but each part of any petition shall have attached thereto the affidavit of the person circulating the same, that all signatures thereon were made in the presence of the affiant, and that to the best of the affiant's knowledge and belief each signature is genuine, and that the person signing is a legal voter and no other affidavit or verification shall be required to establish the genuineness of such signatures.

Sufficiency.
The sufficiency of all state-wide petitions shall be decided in the first instance by the Secretary of State, subject to review by the Supreme Court of the State, which shall have original and exclusive jurisdiction over all such causes. The sufficiency of all local petitions shall be decided in the first instance by the county clerk or the city clerk as the case may be, subject to review by the chancery court. Court Decisions. If the sufficiency of any petition is challenged such cause shall be a preference cause and shall be tried at once, but the failure of the courts to decide prior to the election as to the sufficiency of any such petition, shall not prevent the question from being placed upon the ballot at the election named in such petition, nor militate against the validity of such measure, if it shall have been approved by a vote of the people. Amendment of Petition. (a)(1) If the Secretary of State, county clerk or city clerk, as the case may be, shall decide any petition to be insufficient, he or she shall without delay notify the sponsors of such petition, and permit at least thirty (30) days from the date of such notification, in the instance of a state-wide petition, or ten (10) days in the instance of a municipal or county petition, for correction or amendment. (2) For a state-wide petition, correction or amendment of an insufficient petition shall be permitted only if the petition contains valid signatures of legal voters equal to: (A) At least seventy-five percent (75%) of the number of state-wide signatures of legal voters required; and (B) At least seventy-five percent (75%) of the required number of signatures of legal voters from each of at least fifteen (15)

counties of the state. (b) In the event of legal proceedings to prevent giving legal effect to any petition upon any grounds, the burden of proof shall be upon the person or persons attacking the validity of the petition.

Unwarranted Restrictions Prohibited.
No law shall be passed to prohibit any person or persons from giving or receiving compensation for circulating petitions, nor to prohibit the circulation of petitions, nor in any manner interfering with the freedom of the people in procuring petitions; but laws shall be enacted prohibiting and penalizing perjury, forgery, and all other felonies or other fraudulent practices, in the securing of signatures or filing of petitions.

Publication.
All measures submitted to a vote of the people by petition under the provisions of this section shall be published as is now, or hereafter may be provided by law.

Enacting Clause.
The style of all bills initiated and submitted under the provisions of this section shall be, "Be It Enacted by the People of the State of Arkansas, (municipality or county, as the case may be)." In submitting measures to the people, the Secretary of State and all other officials shall be guided by the general election laws or municipal laws as the case may be until additional legislation is provided therefor. Self-Executing. This section shall be self-executing, and all its provisions shall be treated as mandatory, but laws may be enacted to facilitate its operation. No legislation shall be enacted to restrict, hamper or impair the exercise of the rights herein reserved to the people.

Section 2. House of Representatives.
The House of Representatives shall consist of members to be chosen every second year, by the qualified electors of the several counties.

Section 3. Senate.
The Senate shall consist of members to be chosen every four years, by the qualified electors of the several districts. At the first session of the Senate, the Senators shall divide themselves into two classes, by lot, and the first class shall hold their places for two years only, after which all shall be elected for four years.

Section 4. Qualifications of senators and representatives.
No person shall be a Senator or Representative who, at the time of his election, is not a citizen of the United States, nor any one who has not been for two years next preceding his election, a resident of this State, and for one year next preceding his election, a resident of the county or district whence he may be chosen. Senators shall be at least twenty-five years of age, and Representatives at least twenty-one years of age.

Section 5. Regular and fiscal sessions.
(a) The General Assembly shall meet at the seat of government every year. (b) The General Assembly shall meet in regular session on the second Monday in January of each odd-numbered year to consider any bill or resolution. The General Assembly may alter the time at which the regular session begins. (c)(1) Beginning in 2010, the General Assembly shall meet in fiscal session on the second Monday in February of each even-numbered year to consider only appropriation bills. The General Assembly may alter the time at which the fiscal session begins. (2) A bill other than an appropriation bill may be considered in a fiscal session if two-thirds (2/3) of the members of each house of the General Assembly approve consideration of the bill. (d) The General Assembly, by a vote of two-thirds (2/3) of the members elected to each house of the General Assembly, may alter the dates of the regular session and fiscal session so that regular sessions occur in even numbered years and the fiscal sessions occur in odd-numbered years.

Section 6. Vacancies — Writs of election.
The Governor shall issue writs of election, to fill such vacancies as shall occur in either house of the General Assembly.

Section 7. Officers ineligible.
No judge of the Supreme, Circuit or inferior courts of law or equity, Secretary of State, Attorney General for the State, Auditor or Treasurer, Recorder, clerk of any court of record, Sheriff, Coroner, member of Congress, nor any other person holding any lucrative office under the United States or this State (militia officers, justices of the peace, postmasters, officers of public schools and notaries excepted), shall be eligible to a seat in either house of the General Assembly.

Section 8. Defaulters ineligible.
No person who now is, or shall be hereafter, a collector or holder of public money, nor any assistant or deputy of such holder or collector of public money, shall be eligible to a seat in either house of the General Assembly, nor to any office of trust or profit, until he shall have accounted for, and paid over, all sums for which he may have been liable.

Section 9. Persons convicted ineligible.
No person hereafter convicted of embezzlement of public money, bribery, forgery or other infamous crime, shall be eligible to the General Assembly or capable of holding any office of trust or profit in this State.

Section 10. Members ineligible to civil office.
No Senator or Representative shall, during the term for which he shall have been elected, be appointed or elected to any civil office under this State.

Section 11. Appointment of officers — Qualifications of members — Quorum.

Each house shall appoint its own officers, and shall be sole judge of the qualifications, returns and elections of its own members. A majority of all the members elected to each house shall constitute a quorum to do business; but a smaller number may adjourn from day to day, and compel the attendance of absent members, in such manner and under such penalties as each house shall provide.

Section 12. Powers and duties of each house.

Each house shall have power to determine the rules of its proceedings; and punish its members, or other persons, for contempt or disorderly behavior in its presence; enforce obedience to its process; to protect its members against violence or offers of bribes, or private solicitations; and, with the concurrence of two-thirds, expel a member; but not a second time for the same cause. A member expelled for corruption shall not, thereafter, be eligible to either house; and punishment for contempt, or disorderly behavior, shall not bar an indictment for the same offense. Each house shall keep a journal of its proceedings; and, from time to time, publish the same, except such parts as require secrecy; and the yeas and nays, on any question, shall, at the desire of any five members, be entered on the journals.

Section 13. Sessions to be open.

The sessions of each house, and of committees of the whole, shall be open, unless when the business is such as ought to be kept secret.

Section 14. Election of officers by General Assembly.

Whenever an officer, civil or military, shall be appointed by the joint or concurrent vote of both houses, or by the separate vote of either house of the General Assembly, the vote shall be taken viva voce, and entered on the journals.

Section 15. Privileges of members.
The members of the General Assembly shall, in all cases except treason, felony, and breach or surety of the peace, be privileged from arrest during their attendance at the sessions of their respective houses; and, in going to and returning from the same; and, for any speech or debate in either house, they shall not be questioned in any other place.

Section 16.

Repealed.

Section 17. Duration of sessions.
(a) A regular biennial session shall not exceed sixty (60) calendar days in duration, unless extended by a vote of two-thirds (2/3) of the members elected to each house of the General Assembly. The regular biennial session shall not exceed seventy five (75) calendar days in duration, unless extended by a vote of three-fourths (3/4) of the members elected to each house of the General Assembly. (b) A fiscal session shall not exceed thirty (30) calendar days in duration, except that by a vote of three-fourths (3/4) of the members elected to each house of the General Assembly a fiscal session may be extended one (1) time by no more than fifteen (15) calendar days. (c) Provided, that this section shall not apply when impeachments are pending.

Section 18. Presiding officers.
Each house, at the beginning of every regular session of the General Assembly, and whenever a vacancy may occur, shall elect from its members a presiding officer, to be styled, respectively, the President of the Senate, and the Speaker of the House of Representatives; and whenever, at the close of any session, it may appear that the term of the member elected President of the Senate will expire before the next regular session, the Senate shall elect another President from those members whose terms of office continue over, who shall qualify and remain President of the Senate until his successor may be elected and qualified; and who, in the case of a vacancy in the

office of Governor, shall perform the duties and exercise the powers of Governor as elsewhere herein provided.

Section 19. Style of laws — Enacting clause.
The style of the laws of the State of Arkansas shall be: "Be it enacted by the General Assembly of the State of Arkansas."

Section 20. State not made defendant.
The State of Arkansas shall never be made defendant in any of her courts.

Section 21. Laws by bills — Amendment.
No law shall be passed except by bill, and no bill shall be so altered or amended on its passage through either house, as to change its original purpose.

Section 22. Passage of bills.
Every bill shall be read at length, on three different days, in each house; unless the rules be suspended by two-thirds of the house, when the same may be read a second or third time on the same day; and no bill shall become a law unless, on its final passage, the vote be taken by yeas and nays; the names of the persons voting for and against the same be entered on the journal; and a majority of each house be recorded thereon as voting in its favor.

Section 23. Revival, amendment or extension of laws.
No law shall be revived, amended, or the provisions thereof extended or conferred, by reference to its title only; but so much thereof as is revived, amended, extended or conferred, shall be reenacted and published at length.

Section 24. Local and special laws.
The General Assembly shall not pass any local or special law, changing the venue in criminal cases; changing the names of persons, or adopting or legitimating children; granting divorces; vacating roads, streets or alleys.

Section 25. Special laws — Suspension of general laws.
In all cases where a general law can be made applicable, no special law shall be enacted; nor shall the operation of any general law be suspended by the legislature for the benefit of any particular individual, corporation or association; nor where the courts have jurisdiction to grant the powers, or the privileges, or the relief asked for.

Section 26. Notice of local or special bills.
No local or special bill shall be passed, unless notice of the intention to apply therefor shall have been published, in the locality where the matter or the thing to be affected may be situated; which notice shall be, at least, thirty days prior to the introduction into the General Assembly of such bill, and in the manner to be provided by law. The evidence of such notice having been published, shall be exhibited in the General Assembly before such act shall be passed.

Section 27. Extra compensation prohibited — Exception.
No extra compensation shall be made to any officer, agent, employee, or contractor, after the service shall have been rendered, or the contract made; nor shall any money be appropriated or paid on any claim, the subject matter of which shall not have been provided for by preexisting laws; unless such compensation, or claim, be allowed by bill passed by two-thirds of the members elected to each branch of the General Assembly.

Section 28. Adjournments.
Neither house shall, without the consent of the other, adjourn for more than three days; nor to any other place than that in which the two houses shall be sitting.

Section 29. Appropriations.
Except as provided in Arkansas Constitution, Article 19, Section 31, no money shall be drawn from the treasury except in pursuance of specific appropriation made by law, the purpose of which shall be distinctly stated in the bill, and the maximum amount which may be drawn shall be specified in dollars and

cents; and no appropriations made by the General Assembly after December 31, 2008, shall be for a longer period than one (1) fiscal year.

Section 30. General and special appropriations.
Except as provided in Arkansas Constitution, Article 19, Section 31, the general appropriation bill shall embrace nothing but appropriations for the ordinary expenses of the executive, legislative and judicial departments of the State; all other appropriations shall be made by separate bills, each embracing but one subject.

Section 31. Purposes of taxes and appropriations.
No State tax shall be allowed, or appropriation of money made, except to raise means for the payment of the just debts of the State, for defraying the necessary expenses of government, to sustain common schools, to repel invasion and suppress insurrection, except by a majority of two-thirds of both houses of the General Assembly.

Section 32. Workmen's Compensation Laws — Actions for personal injuries.
The General Assembly shall have power to enact laws prescribing the amount of compensation to be paid by employers for injuries to or death of employees, and to whom said payment shall be made. It shall have power to provide the means, methods, and forum for adjudicating claims arising under said laws, and for securing payment of same. Provided, that otherwise no law shall be enacted limiting the amount to be recovered for injuries resulting in death or for injuries to persons or property; and in case of death from such injuries the right of action shall survive, and the General Assembly shall prescribe for whose benefit such action shall be prosecuted.

Section 33. Liabilities of corporations to state.
No obligation or liability of any railroad, or other corporation, held or owned by this State shall ever be exchanged, transferred, remitted, postponed or in any way diminished by the General Assembly; nor shall such liability or obligation be released, except by payment thereof into the State treasury.

Section 34. Introduction of bills — Time limit.
No new bill shall be introduced into either house during the last three days of a regular or fiscal session.

Section 35. Bribery of member of General Assembly or state officer.
Any person who shall, directly or indirectly, offer, give, or promise any money, or thing of value, testimonial, privilege or personal advantage to any executive or judicial officer, or member of the General Assembly; and any such executive or judicial officer, or member of the General Assembly, who shall receive or consent to receive any such consideration, either directly or ndirectly, to influence his action in the performance or non performance of his public or official duty, shall be guilty of a felony, and be punished accordingly.

Section 36. Expulsion of member no bar to indictment.
Proceedings to expel a member for a criminal offense, whether successful or not, shall not bar an indictment and punishment, under the criminal laws, for the same offense.

Section 37. Laws — Enactment — Majority required.
Not less than a majority of the members of each House of the General Assembly may enact a law.

Section 38. Taxes — Increase — Approval by electors.
None of the rates for property, excise, privilege or personal taxes, now levied shall be increased by the General Assembly except after the approval of the qualified electors voting thereon at an election, or in case of emergency, by the votes of three-fourths of the members elected to each House of the General

Assembly.

Section 39. State expenses — Limitation — Exceptions.
Excepting monies raised or collected for educational purposes, highway purposes, to pay Confederate pensions and the just debts of the State, the General Assembly is hereby prohibited from appropriating or expending more than the sum of Two and One-Half Million Dollars for all purposes, for any fiscal year; provided the limit herein fixed may be exceeded by the votes of three-fourths of the members elected to each House of the General Assembly.

Section 40. General appropriation bill — Enactment.
In making appropriations for any fiscal year, the General Assembly shall first pass the General Appropriation Bill provided for in Section 30 of Article 5 of the Constitution, and no other appropriation bill may be enacted before that shall have been done.

Section 41. Expenses incurred or authorized only by bill — Repealing clause. Section 5.
No expense shall be incurred or authorized for either House except by a bill duly passed by both Houses and approved by the Governor.

Section 42. Review and approval of administrative rules.
(a) The General Assembly may provide by law: (1) For the review by a legislative committee of administrative rules promulgated by a state agency before the administrative rules become effective; and   (2) That administrative rules promulgated by a state agency shall not become effective until reviewed and approved by the legislative committee charged by law with the review of administrative rules under subdivision (a)(1) of this section.
(b) The review and approval by a legislative committee under subsection (a) of this section may occur during the interim or during a regular, special, or fiscal session of the General Assembly.

Article VI: Executive Department

Section 1. Executive officers.
The executive department of this State shall consist of a Governor, Lieutenant Governor, Secretary of State, Treasurer of State, Auditor of State and Attorney General, all of whom shall keep their offices in person at the seat of government and hold their offices for the term of two years and until their successors are elected and qualified, and the General Assembly may provide by law for the establishment of the office of Commissioner of State Lands.

Section 2. Governor — Supreme executive power.
The supreme executive power of this State shall be vested in a chief magistrate, who shall be styled "the Governor of the State of Arkansas."

Section 3. Election of executive officers.
The Governor, Secretary of State, Treasurer of State, Auditor of State, and Attorney General shall be elected by the qualified electors of the State at large, at the time and places of voting for members of the General Assembly; the returns of each election therefor shall be sealed up separately and transmitted to the seat of government by the returning officers, and directed to the Speaker of the House of Representatives; who shall, during the first week of the session, open and publish the votes cast and given for each of the respective officers hereinbefore mentioned, in the presence of both houses of the General Assembly. The person having the highest number of votes, for each of the respective offices, shall be declared duly elected thereto; but if two or more shall be equal, and highest in votes for the same office, one of them shall be chosen by the joint vote of both houses of the General Assembly, and a majority of all the members elected shall be necessary to a choice.

Section 4. Contested election.
Contested elections for Governor, Secretary of State, Treasurer of State, Auditor of State, and Attorney General shall be determined by the members of both houses of the General Assembly, in joint session; who shall have exclusive jurisdiction in trying and determining the same, except as hereinafter provided in the case of special elections; and all such contests shall be tried and determined at the first session of the General Assembly after the election in which the same shall have arisen.

Section 5. Qualifications of Governor.
No person shall be eligible to the office of Governor except a citizen of the United States, who shall have attained the age of thirty years, and shall have been seven years a resident of this State.

Section 6. Governor, commander-in-chief of armed services.
The Governor shall be commander-in-chief of the military and naval forces of this State, except when they shall be called into the actual service of the United States.

Section 7. Information and reports from departments.
He may require information, in writing, from the officers of the executive department, on any subject relating to the duties of their respective offices; and shall see that the laws are faithfully executed.

Section 8. Messages to General Assembly.
He shall give to the General Assembly, from time to time, and at the close of his official term, to the next General Assembly, information, by message, concerning the condition and government of the State; and recommend for their consideration such measures as he may deem expedient.

Section 9. Seal of State.
A seal of the State shall be kept by the Governor, used by him officially, and called the "Great Seal of the State of Arkansas."

Section 10. Grants and commissions.

All grants and commissions shall be issued in the name, and by the authority, of the State of Arkansas; sealed with the great seal of the State; signed by the Governor, and attested by the Secretary of State.

Section 11. Incompatible offices.
No member of Congress, or other person holding office under the authority of this State, or of the United States, shall exercise the office of Governor, except as herein provided.

Section 12. President of Senate succeeding to Governor's office.
In case of the death, conviction on impeachment, failure to qualify, resignation, absence from the State, or other disability of the Governor, the powers, duties and emoluments of the office for the remainder of the term, or until the disability be removed, or a Governor elected and qualified, shall devolve upon, and accrue, to the President of the Senate.

Section 13. Speaker of House succeeding to office of Governor.
If, during the vacancy of the office of Governor, the President of the Senate shall be impeached, removed from office, refuse to qualify, resign, die, or be absent from the State; the Speaker of the House of Representatives shall, in like manner, administer the government.

Section 14. Election to fill vacancy.
Whenever the office of Governor shall have become vacant by death, resignation, removal from office or otherwise, provided such vacancy shall not happen within twelve months next before the expiration of the term of office for which the late Governor

shall have been elected, the President of the Senate or Speaker of the House of Representatives, as the case may be, exercising the powers of Governor for the time being, shall immediately cause an election to be held to fill such vacancy, giving, by proclamation, sixty days, previous notice thereof, which election shall be governed by the same rules prescribed for general elections of Governor as far as applicable; the returns shall be made to the Secretary of State, and the acting Governor, Secretary of State and Attorney General shall constitute a board of canvassers, a majority of whom shall compare said returns and declare who is elected; and if there be a contested election, it shall be decided as may be provided by law.

Section 15. Approval of bills — Vetoes.
Every bill which shall have passed both houses of the General Assembly, shall be presented to the Governor; if he approve it, he shall sign it; but if he shall not approve it, he shall return it, with his objections, to the house in which it originated; which house shall enter the objections at large upon their journal and proceed to reconsider it. If, after such reconsideration, a majority of the whole number elected to that house, shall agree to pass the bill, it shall be sent, with the objections, to the other house; by which, likewise, it shall be reconsidered; and, if approved by a majority of the whole number elected to that house, it shall be a law; but in such cases the vote of both houses shall be determined by "yeas and nays;" and the names of the members voting for or against the bill, shall be entered on the journals. If any bill shall not be returned by the Governor within five days, Sundays excepted, after it shall have been presented to him, the same shall be a law in like manner as if he had signed it; unless the General Assembly, by their adjournment, prevent its return; in which case it shall become a law, unless he shall file the same, with his objections, in the office of the Secretary of State, and give notice thereof, by public proclamation, within twenty days after such adjournment.

Section 16. Concurrent orders or resolutions — Veto.

Every order or resolution in which the concurrence of both houses of the General Assembly may be necessary, except on questions of adjournment, shall be presented to the Governor, and, before it shall take effect, be approved by him; or, being disapproved, shall be repassed by both houses according to the rules and limitations prescribed in the case of a bill.

Section 17. Vetoes of items of appropriation bills.

The Governor shall have power to disapprove any item, or items, of any bill making appropriation of money, embracing distinct items; and the part or parts of the bill approved shall be the law; and the item or items of appropriations disapproved, shall be void unless repassed according to the rules and limitations prescribed for the passage of other bills over the executive veto.

Section 18. Pardoning power.

In all criminal and penal cases, except in those of treason and impeachment, the Governor shall have power to grant reprieves, commutations of sentence, and pardons, after conviction; and to remit fines and forfeitures, under such rules and regulations as shall be prescribed by law. In cases of treason, he shall have power, by and with the advice and consent of the Senate, to grant reprieves and pardons; and he may, in the recess of the Senate, respite the sentence until the adjournment of the next regular session of the General Assembly. He shall communicate to the General Assembly at every regular session each case of reprieve, commutation or pardon, with his reasons therefor; stating the name and crime of the convict, the sentence, its date, and the date of the commutation, pardon or reprieve.

Section 19. Extraordinary sessions of General Assembly — Calling — Purposes.

The Governor may, by proclamation, on extraordinary occasions, convene the General Assembly at the seat of government, or at a different place, if that shall have become, since their last adjournment, dangerous from an enemy or contagious disease; and he shall specify in his proclamation the purpose for which they are convened; and no other business than that set forth therein shall be transacted until the same shall have been disposed of; after which they may, by a vote of two-thirds of all the members elected to both houses, entered upon their journals, remain in session not exceeding fifteen days.

Section 20. Power to adjourn General Assembly.
In cases of disagreement between the two houses of the General Assembly, at a regular or special session, with respect to the time of adjournment, the Governor may, if the facts be certified to him by the presiding officers of the two houses, adjourn them to a time not beyond the day of their next meeting; and on account of danger from an enemy or disease, to such other place of safety as he may think proper.

Section 21. Duties of Secretary of State.
The Secretary of State shall keep a full and accurate record of all the official acts and proceedings of the Governor; and, when required, lay the same with all papers, minutes and vouchers relating thereto, before either branch of the General Assembly. He shall also discharge the duties of Superintendent of Public Instruction, until otherwise provided by law.

Section 22. Duties of executive officers in general — Dual office holding prohibited — Vacancies — Filling.
The Treasurer of State, Secretary of State, Auditor of State, and Attorney-General shall perform such duties as may be prescribed by law; they shall not hold any other office or commission, civil or military, in this State or under any State, or the United States, or any other power, at one and the same time; and in case of vacancy occurring in any of said offices, by death, resignation or otherwise, the Governor shall fill said office by appointment for the unexpired term.

Section 23. Filling vacancies in other offices.
When any office, from any cause, may become vacant, and no mode is provided by the Constitution and laws for filling such vacancy, the Governor shall have the power to fill the same by granting a commission, which shall expire when the person elected to fill said office, at the next general election, shall be duly qualified.

Article VII: Judicial Department

Section 1 — 18.

Repealed.

Section 19. Circuit clerks — Election — Term of office — Ex-officio duties — County clerks elected in certain counties.
The clerks of the circuit courts shall be elected by the qualified electors of the several counties for the term of two years, and shall be ex-officio clerks of the county and probate courts and recorder; provided, that in any county having a population exceeding fifteen thousand inhabitants, as shown by the last Federal census, there shall be elected a county clerk, in like manner as the clerk of the circuit court, and in such case the county clerk shall be ex-officio clerk of the probate court of such county until otherwise provided by the General Assembly.

Section 20 — 22.

Repealed.

Section 23. Charge to juries.
Judges shall not charge juries with regard to matters of fact, but shall declare the law; and, in jury trials, shall reduce their charge or instructions to writing, on the request of either party.

Section 24.

Repealed.

Section 25.

Repealed.

Section 26. Punishment of indirect contempt provided for by law.

The General Assembly shall have power to regulate, by law, the punishment of contempts; not committed in the presence or hearing of the courts, or in disobedience of process.

Section 27. Removal of county and township officers — Grounds.

The Circuit Court shall have jurisdiction upon information, presentment, or indictment, to remove any county or township officer from office for incompetency, corruption, gross immorality, criminal conduct, malfeasance, misfeasance or nonfeasance in office.

Section 28. County courts — Jurisdiction — Single judge holding court.

The County Courts shall have exclusive original jurisdiction in all matters relating to county taxes, roads, bridges, ferries, paupers, bastardy, vagrants, the apprenticeship of minors, the disbursement of money for county purposes, and in every other case that may be necessary to the internal improvement and local concerns of the respective counties. The County Court shall be held by one judge, except in cases otherwise herein provided.

Section 29. County judge — Election — Term — Qualifications.

The Judge of the County Court shall be elected by the qualified electors of the county for the term of two years. He shall be at least twenty-five years of age, a citizen of the United States, a man of upright character, of good business education, and a resident of the State for two years before his election; and a resident of the county at the time of his election, and during his continuance in office. The Justices of the Peace of each county shall sit with and assist the County Judge in levying the county taxes, and in making appropriations for the expenses of the county, in the manner to be prescribed by law; and the County Judge, together with a majority of said Justices, shall constitute a quorum for such purposes; and in the absence of the County Judge a majority of the Justices of the Peace may constitute the court, who shall elect one of their number to preside. The General Assembly shall regulate by law the manner of compelling the attendance of such quorum.

Section 31. County court — Terms.
The terms of the County Courts shall be held at the times that are now prescribed for holding the Supervisors' Courts, or may hereafter be prescribed by law.

Section 32.

Repealed.

Section 33. Appeals from county and common pleas courts.
Appeals from all judgments of County Courts or Courts of Common Pleas, when established, may be taken to the Circuit Court under such restrictions and regulations as may be prescribed by law.

Section 34.

Repealed.

Section 35.

Repealed.

Section 36. Special judges of county or probate courts.
Whenever a Judge of the County or Probate Court may be disqualified from presiding, in any cause or causes pending in his court, he shall certify the facts to the Governor of the State, who shall thereupon commission a special judge to preside in such cause or causes during the time said disqualification may continue, or until such cause or causes may be finally disposed of.

Section 37. Compensation of county judge — Powers during absence of circuit judge.
The County Judge shall receive such compensation for his services as presiding Judge of the County Court, as Judge of the Court of Probate and Judge of the Court of Common Pleas, when established, as may be provided by law. In the absence of the Circuit Judge from the county, the County Judge shall have power to issue orders for injunctions and other provisional writs in their counties, returnable to the court having jurisdiction; provided, that either party may have such order reviewed by any superior Judge in vacation in such manner as shall be provided by law. The County Judge shall have power, in the absence of the Circuit Judge from the county, to issue, hear and determine writs of habeas corpus, under such regulations and restrictions as shall be provided by law.

Section 38. Justices of the peace — Election — Term — Oath. The qualified electors of each township shall elect the Justices of the Peace for the term of two years; who shall be commissioned by the Governor, and their official oath shall be endorsed on the commission.

Section 39.

Repealed.

Section 40.

Repealed.

Section 41. Qualifications of justice of peace. A Justice of the Peace shall be a qualified elector and a resident of the township for which he is elected.

Section 42.

Repealed.

Section 43.

Repealed.

Section 44.

Repealed.

Section 45.

Repealed.

Section 46. County executive officers — Compensation of county assessor.
The qualified electors of each county shall elect one Sheriff, who shall be ex-officio collector of taxes, unless otherwise provided by law; one Assessor, one Coroner, one Treasurer, who shall be ex-officio treasurer of the common school fund of the county, and one County Surveyor; for the term of two years, with such duties as are now or may be prescribed by law: Provided, that no per centum shall ever be paid to assessors upon the valuation or assessment of property by them.

Section 47. Constables — Term of office — Certificate of election.
The qualified electors of each township shall elect the Constable for the term of two years, who shall be furnished, by the presiding Judge of the County Court, with a certificate of election, on which his official oath shall be endorsed.

Section 48. Commissions of officers. All officers provided for in this article, except Constables, shall be commissioned by the Governor.

Section 49. Style of process and of indictments.

All writs and other judicial process, shall run in the name of the State of Arkansas, bear test and be signed by the clerks of the respective courts from which they issue. Indictments shall conclude: "Against the peace and dignity of the State of Arkansas."

Section 50.

Repealed.

Section 51. Appeals from county or municipal allowances — Bond.

That in all cases of allowances made for or against counties, cities or towns, an appeal shall lie to the Circuit Court of the county, at the instance of the party aggrieved, or on the intervention of any citizen or resident and tax payer of such county, city or town, on the same terms and conditions on which appeals may be granted to the Circuit Court in other cases; and the matter pertaining to any such allowance shall be tried in the Circuit Court de novo. In case an appeal be taken by any citizen, he shall give a bond, payable to the proper county, conditioned to prosecute the appeal, and save the county from costs on account of the same being taken.

Section 52. Appeals in election contests.

That in all cases of contest for any county, township, or municipal office, an appeal shall lie at the instance of the party aggrieved, from any inferior board, council, or tribunal to the Circuit Court, on the same terms and conditions on which appeals may be granted to the Circuit Court in other cases, and on such appeals the case shall be tried de novo.

Article VIII: Apportionment
Membership in General Assembly

Section 1. Board of apportionment created — Powers and duties.

A Board to be known as "The Board of Apportionment," consisting of the Governor (who shall be Chairman), the Secretary of State and the Attorney General is hereby created and it shall be its imperative duty to make apportionment of representatives in accordance with the provisions hereof; the action of a majority in each instance shall be deemed the action of said board.

Section 2. One hundred members in House of Representatives — Apportionment.

The House of Representatives shall consist of one hundred members and each county existing at the time of any apportionment shall have at least one representative; the remaining members shall be equally distributed (as nearly as practicable) among the more populous counties of the State, in accordance with a ratio to be determined by the population of said counties as shown by the Federal census next preceding any apportionment hereunder.

Section 3. Senatorial districts — Thirty-five members of Senate.

The Senate shall consist of thirty-five members. Senatorial districts shall at all times consist of contiguous territory, and no county shall be divided in the formation of such districts. "The Board of Apportionment" hereby created shall, from time to time, divide the state into convenient senatorial districts in such manner as that the Senate shall be based upon the inhabitants of the state, each senator representing, as nearly as practicable, an equal number thereof; each district shall have at least one senator.

Section 4. Duties of Board of Apportionment.

On or before February 1 immediately following each Federal census, said board shall reapportion the State for Representatives, and in each instance said board shall file its report with the Secretary of State, setting forth (a) the basis of population adopted for representatives; (b) the number of representatives assigned to each county; whereupon, after 30 days from such filing date, the apportionment thus made shall become effective unless proceedings for revision be instituted in the Supreme Court within said period.

Section 5. Mandamus to compel Board of Apportionment to act.

Original jurisdiction (to be exercised on application of any citizens and taxpayers) is hereby vested in the Supreme Court of the State (a) to compel (by mandamus or otherwise) the board to perform its duties as here directed and (b) to revise any arbitrary action of or abuse of discretion by the board in making such apportionment; provided any such application for revision shall be filed with said Court within 30 days after the filing of the report of apportionment by said board with the Secretary of State; if revised by the court, a certified copy of its judgment shall be by the clerk thereof forthwith transmitted to the Secretary of State, and thereupon be and become a substitute for the apportionment made by the board.

Section 6. Election of Senators and Representatives.

At the next general election for State and County officers ensuing after any such apportionment, Representatives shall be elected in accordance therewith, Senators shall be elected henceforth according to the apportionment now existing, and their respective terms of office shall begin on January 1 next following. Senators shall be elected for a term of four years at the expiration of their present terms of office.

Article IX: Exemption

Section 1. Personal property exemptions of persons not heads of families.

The personal property of any resident of this State, who is not married or the head of a family, in specific articles to be selected by such resident, not exceeding in value the sum of two hundred dollars, in addition to his or her wearing apparel, shall be exempt from seizure on attachment, or sale on execution or other process from any court, issued for the collection of any debt by contract: Provided, That no property shall be exempt from execution for debts contracted for the purchase money therefor while in the hands of the vendee.

Section 2. Heads of families — Exempt personal property.

The personal property of any resident of this State, who is married or the head of a family, in specific articles to be selected by such resident, not exceeding in value the sum of five hundred dollars, in addition to his or her wearing apparel, and that of his or her family, shall be exempt from seizure on attachment, or sale on execution or other process from any court, on debt by contract.

Section 3. Homestead exemption from legal process — Exceptions.

The homestead of any resident of this State, who is married or the head of a family, shall not be subject to the lien of any judgment or decree of any court, or to sale under execution, or other process thereon, except such as may be rendered for the purchase money, or for specific liens, laborers' or mechanics' liens for improving the same, or for taxes, or against executors, administrators, guardians, receivers, attorneys for moneys collected by them, and other trustees of an express trust, for moneys due from them in their fiduciary capacity.

Section 4. Rural homestead — Acreage — Value.
The homestead outside any city, town or village, owned and occupied as a residence, shall consist of not exceeding one hundred and sixty acres of land, with the improvements thereon, to be selected by the owner; Provided, The same shall not exceed in value the sum of twenty-five hundred dollars, and in no event shall the homestead be reduced to less than eighty acres, without regard to value.

Section 5. Urban homestead — Acreage — Value.
The homestead in any city, town or village, owned and occupied as a residence, shall consist of not exceeding one acre of land, with the improvements thereon, to be selected by the owner; provided, the same shall not exceed in value the sum of two thousand five hundred dollars, and in no event shall such homestead be reduced to less than one-quarter of an acre of land, without regard to value.

Section 6. Rights of widow and children.
If the owner of a homestead die, leaving a widow, but no children, and said widow has no separate homestead in her own right, the same shall be exempt, and the rents and profits thereof shall vest in her during her natural life; Provided, That if the owner leaves children, one or more, said child or children shall share with said widow, and be entitled to half the rents and profits till each of them arrives at twenty-one years of age — each child's rights to cease at twenty-one years of age — and the shares to go to the younger children; and then all to go to the widow; and, provided, that said widow or children may reside on the homestead or not. And in case of the death of the widow, all of said homestead shall be vested in the minor children of the testator or intestate.

Section 7. Married woman's separate property — Right of disposition — Not liable for debts of husband.
The real and personal property of any femme covert in this State, acquired either before or after marriage, whether by gift, grant, inheritance, devise or otherwise, shall, so long as she may choose, be and remain her separate estate and property, and may be devised, bequeathed or conveyed by her the same as if she were a femme sole; and the same shall not be subject to the debts of her husband.

Section 8. Scheduling separate personal property of wife.
The General Assembly shall provide for the time and mode of scheduling the separate personal property of married women.

Section 9. Exemptions under Constitution of 1868 — Existing obligations.
The exemptions contained in the Constitution of 1868 shall apply to all debts contracted since the adoption thereof, and prior to the adoption of this Constitution.

Section 10. Homestead rights of minor children.
The homestead provided for in this article shall inure to the benefit of the minor children, under the exemptions herein provided, after the decease of the parents.

Article X: Agriculture, Mining and Manufacture

Section 1. Mining, manufacturing and agricultural bureau — State aid.
The General Assembly shall pass such laws as will foster and aid the agricultural, mining and manufacturing interests of the State, and may create a bureau, to be known as the Mining, Manufacturing and Agricultural Bureau.

Section 2. State geologist — Creation of office — Appointment and removal.
The General Assembly, when deemed expedient, may create the office of State Geologist, to be appointed by the Governor, by and with the advice and consent of the Senate, who shall hold his office for such time, and perform such duties, and receive such compensation as may be prescribed by law; Provided: That he shall be at all times subject to removal by the Governor, for incompetency or gross neglect of duty.

Section 3. Exemption of mines and manufactures from taxation.
The General Assembly may, by general law, exempt from taxation for the term of seven years from the ratification of this Constitution, the capital invested in any or all kinds of mining and manufacturing business in this State, under such regulations and restrictions as may be prescribed by law.

Article XI: Militia

Section 1. Persons liable to military duty.
The militia shall consist of all able-bodied male persons, residents of the State, between the ages of eighteen and forty-five years; except such as may be exempted by the laws of the United States, or this State; and shall be organized, officered, armed and equipped and trained in such manner as may be provided by law.

Section 2. Volunteer companies.
Volunteer Companies of Infantry, Cavalry or Artillery may be formed in such manner and with such restrictions as may be provided by law.

Section 3. Privilege of members from arrest.
The volunteer and militia forces shall in all cases (except treason, felony and breach of the peace) be privileged from arrest during their attendance at muster and the election of officers, and in going to and returning from the same.

Section 4. Authority to call out volunteers or militia.
The Governor shall, when the General Assembly is not in session, have power to call out the Volunteers or Militia, or both, to execute the laws, repel invasion, repress insurrection and preserve the public peace; in such manner as may be authorized by law.

Article XII: Municipal and Private Corporations

Section 1. Revocation of certain charters.
All existing charters or grants of special or exclusive privileges, under a bona fide organization shall not have taken place, and business been commenced in good faith, at the time of the adoption of this Constitution, shall thereafter have no validity.

Section 2. Special acts prohibited — Exception.
The General Assembly shall pass no special act conferring corporate powers, except for charitable, educational, penal or reformatory purposes, where the corporations created are to be and remain under the patronage and control of the state.

Section 3. Cities and towns — Organization under general laws.
The General Assembly shall provide, by general laws, for the organization of cities (which may be classified) and incorporated towns; and restrict their power of taxation, assessment, borrowing money and contracting debts, so as to prevent the abuse of such power.

Section 4. Limitation on legislative and taxing power — Local bond issues.
No municipal corporation shall be authorized to pass any laws contrary to the general laws of the state; nor levy any tax on real or personal property to a greater extent, in one year, than five mills on the dollar of the assessed value of the same; Provided: That, to pay indebtedness existing at the time of the adoption of this Constitution, an additional tax of not more than five mills on the dollar, may be levied. The fiscal affairs of counties, cities and incorporated towns shall be conducted on a sound financial basis, and no county court or levying board or agent of any county shall make or authorize any contract or make any allowance for any purpose whatsoever in excess of the revenue from all sources for the fiscal year in which said contract or allowance is made; nor shall any county judge, county clerk, or other county officer, sign or issue any scrip warrant or make any

allowance in excess of the revenue from all sources for the current fiscal year; nor shall any city council, board of aldermen, board of public affairs, or commissioners, of any city of the first or second class, or any incorporated town, enter into any contract or make any allowance for any purpose whatsoever, or authorize the issuance of any contract or warrants, scrip or other evidences of indebtedness in excess of the revenue for such city or town for the current fiscal year; nor shall any mayor, city clerk, or recorder, or any other officer or officers, however designated, of any city of the first or second class or incorporated town sign or issue scrip, warrant or other certificate of indebtedness of excess of the revenue from all sources for the current fiscal year. Provided, however, to secure funds to pay indebtedness outstanding at the time of the adoption of this amendment, counties, cities, and incorporated towns may issue interest bearing certificates of indebtedness or bonds with interest coupons for the payment of which a county or city tax, in addition to that now authorized, not exceeding three mills may be levied for the time as provided by law until such indebtedness is paid. Where the annual report of any city or county in the State of Arkansas shows that scrip, warrants or other certificate of indebtedness had been issued in excess of the total revenue for that year, the officer or officers of the county or city or incorporated town who authorized, signed or issued such scrip, warrants or other certificates of indebtedness shall be deemed guilty of a misdemeanor and upon conviction thereof, shall be fined in any sum not less than five hundred dollars nor more than ten thousand dollars, and shall be removed from office.

Section 5. Political subdivisions not to become stockholders in or lend credit to private corporations.

No county, city, town or other municipal corporation, shall become a stockholder in any company, association, or corporation; or obtain or appropriate money for, or loan its credit to, any corporation, association, institution or individual.

Section 6. General incorporation laws — Charters — Revocation.

Corporations may be formed under general laws; which laws may, from time to time, be altered or repealed. The General Assembly shall have the power to alter, revoke or annul any charter of incorporation now existing and revocable at the adoption of this Constitution, or any that may hereafter be created, whenever, in their opinion, it may be injurious to the citizens of this State; in such manner, however, that no injustice shall be done to the corporators.

Section 7. State not to be stockholder.

Except as herein provided, the State shall never become a stockholder in, or subscribe to, or be interested in the stock of any corporation or association.

Section 8. Private corporations — Issuance of stocks or bonds — Conditions and restrictions.

No private corporation shall issue stocks or bonds, except for money or property actually received, or labor done; and all fictitious increase of stock or indebtedness shall be void; nor shall the stock or bonded indebtedness of any private corporation be increased, except in pursuance of general laws; nor until the consent of the persons holding the larger amount, in value, of stock, shall be obtained at a meeting held after notice given, for a period not less than sixty days, in pursuance of law.

Section 9. Taking of property by corporation — Compensation.

No property, nor right of way, shall be appropriated to the use of any corporation, until full compensation therefor shall be first made to the owner, in money; or first secured to him by a deposit of money; which compensation, irrespective of any benefit from any improvement
proposed by such corporation, shall be ascertained by a jury of twelve men, in a court of competent jurisdiction, as shall be prescribed by law.

Section 10. Issue of circulating paper.
No act of the General Assembly shall be passed authorizing the issue of bills, notes, or other paper which may circulate as money.

Section 11. Foreign corporations doing business in state.
Foreign corporations may be authorized to do business in this State, under such limitations and restrictions as may be prescribed by law; Provided: That no such corporation shall do any business in this State, except while it maintains therein one or more known places of business, and an authorized agent or agents in the same, upon whom process may be served; and, as to contracts made or business done in this State, they shall be subject to the same regulations, limitations and liabilities as like corporations of this State; and shall exercise no other or greater powers, privileges or franchises than may be exercised by like corporations of this State; nor shall they have power to condemn or appropriate private property.

Section 12. State not to assume liabilities of political subdivisions or private corporations — Indebtedness to state — Release.
Except as herein otherwise provided, the State shall never assume, or pay the debt or liability of any county, town, city or other corporation whatever; or any part thereof; unless such debt or liability shall have been created to repel invasion, suppress insurrection, or to provide for the public welfare and defense. Nor shall the indebtedness of any corporation to the State, ever be released, or in any manner discharged, save by payment into the public treasury.

Article XIII: Counties, County Seats and County Lines

Section 1. Size of counties — Exceptions.
No county now established shall be reduced to an area of less than six hundred square miles, nor to less than five thousand inhabitants: nor shall any new county be established with less than six hundred square miles and five thousand inhabitants: Provided, that this section shall not apply to the counties of Lafayette, Pope and Johnson, nor be so construed as to prevent the General Assembly from changing the line between the counties of Pope and Johnson.

Section 2. Consent of voters to change of county lines.
No part of a county shall be taken off to form a new county, or a part thereof, without the consent of a majority of the voters in such part proposed to be taken off.

Section 3. Change of county seats — Conditions — New counties.
No county seat shall be established or changed without the consent of a majority of the qualified voters of the county to be affected by such change, nor until the place at which it is proposed to establish or change such county seat shall be fully designated: Provided, That in formation of new counties, the county seat may be located temporarily by provisions of law.

Section 4. Lines of new counties — Distance from county seat of adjoining county — Exception.
In the formation of new counties no line thereof shall run within ten miles of the county seat of the county proposed to be divided, except the county seat of Lafayette County.

Section 5. Sebastian County — Districts.
Sebastian County may have two districts and two county seats, at which county, probate and circuit courts shall be held as may be provided by law, each district paying its own expenses.

Article XIV: Education

Section 1. Free school system.

Intelligence and virtue being the safeguards of liberty and the bulwark of a free and good government, the State shall ever maintain a general, suitable and efficient system of free public schools and shall adopt all suitable means to secure to the people the advantages and opportunities of education. The specific intention of this amendment is to authorize that in addition to existing constitutional or statutory provisions the General Assembly and/or public school districts may spend public funds for the education of persons over twenty-one (21) years of age and under six (6) years of age, as may be provided by law, and no other interpretation shall be given to it.

Section 2. School fund — Use — Purposes.

No money or property belonging to the public school fund, or to this State, for the benefit of schools or universities, shall ever be used for any other than for the respective purposes to which it belongs.

Section 3. School tax — Budget — Approval of tax rate

(a) The General Assembly shall provide for the support of common schools by general law. In order to provide quality education, it is the goal of this state to provide a fair system for the distribution of funds. It is recognized that, in providing such a system, some funding variations may be necessary. The primary reason for allowing such variations is to allow school districts, to the extent permissible, to raise additional funds to enhance the educational system within the school district. It is further recognized that funding variations or restrictions thereon may be necessary in order to comply with, or due to, other provisions of this Constitution, the United States Constitution, state or federal laws, or court orders. (b)(1) There is established a uniform rate of ad valorem property tax of twenty-five (25) mills to be levied on the assessed value of all taxable real, personal, and utility property in the state to be used solely for maintenance and operation of the schools. (2) Except as provided in this subsection the uniform rate of tax shall not be an additional levy for maintenance and operation of the schools but shall replace a portion of the existing rate of tax levied by each school district available for maintenance and operation of schools in the school district. The rate of tax available for maintenance and operation levied by each school district on the effective date of this amendment shall be reduced to reflect the levy of the uniform rate of tax. If the rate of tax available for maintenance and operation levied by a school district on the effective date of this amendment exceeds the uniform rate of tax, the excess rate of tax shall continue to be levied by the school district until changed as provided in subsection (c)(1). If the rate of tax available for maintenance and operation levied by a school district on the effective date of this amendment is less than the uniform rate of tax, the uniform rate of tax shall nevertheless be levied in the district. (3) The uniform rate of tax shall be assessed and collected in the same manner as other school property taxes, but the net revenues from the uniform rate of tax shall be remitted to the State Treasurer and distributed by the state to the school districts as provided by law. No portion of the revenues from the uniform rate of tax shall be retained by the state. The revenues so distributed shall be used by the school districts solely for maintenance and operation of schools. (4) The General Assembly may by law propose an increase or decrease in the uniform rate of tax and submit the question to the electors of the state at the next general election. If a majority of the electors of the state voting on the issue vote For the proposed increase or decrease in the uniform rate of tax, the uniform rate of tax shall be increased or decreased as approved. If a majority of the electors of the state voting on the issue vote Against the proposed increase or decrease in the uniform rate of tax, the uniform rate of tax shall continue to be levied at the rate for the year in which the election is held. (c)(1) In addition to the uniform rate of tax provided in subsection (b), school districts are authorized to levy, by a vote of the qualified electors respectively thereof, an annual ad valorem property tax on the assessed value of taxable real, personal, and utility property for the maintenance and operation of schools and the retirement of indebtedness.

The Board of Directors of each school district shall prepare, approve and make public not less than sixty (60) days in advance of the annual school election a proposed budget of expenditures deemed necessary to provide for the foregoing purposes, together with a rate of tax levy sufficient to provide the funds therefor, including the rate under any continuing levy for the retirement of indebtedness. The Board of Directors shall submit the tax at the annual school election or at such other time as may be provided by law. If a majority of the qualified voters in the school district voting in the school election approve the rate of tax proposed by the Board of Directors, then the tax at the rate approved shall be collected as provided by law. In the event a majority of the qualified electors voting in the school election disapprove the proposed rate of tax, then the tax shall be collected at the rate approved in the last preceding school election. However, if the rate last approved has been modified pursuant to subsection (b) or (c)(2) of this section, then the tax shall be collected at the modified rate until another rate is approved.   (2) The tax levied by a school district pursuant to subsection (c)(1) of this section may be reduced pursuant to procedures provided by law if the tax would cause the state or district to be out of compliance with any other provision of this Constitution, the United States Constitution, state or federal law, or court order.   (3) No tax levied pursuant to subsection (c)(1) of this section shall be appropriated to any other district than that for which it is levied. (d) For the purposes of this section, "maintenance and operation" means such expenses for the general maintenance and operation of schools as may be defined by law.

Section 4. Supervision of schools.
The supervision of public schools, and the execution of the laws regulating the same, shall be vested in and confided to, such officers as may be provided for by the General Assembly.

Article XV: Impeachment and Address

Section 1. Officers subject to impeachment — Grounds.
The Governor and all State officers, Judges of the Supreme and Circuit Courts, Chancellors and Prosecuting Attorneys, shall be liable to impeachment for high crimes and misdemeanors, and gross misconduct in office; but the judgment shall go no further than removal from office and disqualification to hold any office of honor, trust or profit under this State. An impeachment, whether successful or not, shall be no bar to an indictment.

Section 2. Impeachment by House — Trial by Senate — Presiding officer.
The House of Representatives shall have the sole power of impeachment. All impeachments shall be tried by the Senate. When sitting for that purpose, the Senators shall be upon oath or affirmation; no person shall be convicted without the concurrence of two-thirds of the members thereof. The Chief Justice shall preside, unless he is impeached or otherwise disqualified, when the Senate shall select a presiding officer.

Section 3. Officers removable by Governor upon address.
The governor, upon the joint address of two-thirds of all the members elected to each House of the General Assembly, for good cause, may remove the Auditor, Treasurer, Secretary of State, Attorney-General, Judges of the Supreme and Circuit Courts, Chancellors and Prosecuting Attorneys.

Article XVI: Finance and Taxation

Section 1. Lending credit — Bond issues — Interest-bearing warrants.

Neither the State nor any city, county, town or other municipality in this State shall ever lend its credit for any purpose whatever; nor shall any county, city or town or municipality ever issue any interest bearing evidences of indebtedness, except such bonds as may be authorized by law to provide for and secure the payment of the indebtedness existing at the time of the adoption of the Constitution of 1874, and the State shall never issue any interest-bearing treasury warrants or scrip.

Section 2. Debts of state — Payment.

The General Assembly shall, from time to time, provide for the payment of all just and legal debts of the State.

Section 3. Making profit out of or misusing public funds — Penalty.

The making of profit out of public moneys, or using the same for any purpose not authorized by law, by any officer of the State, or member or officer of the General Assembly, shall be punishable as may be provided by law, but part of such punishment shall be disqualification to hold office in this State for a period of five years.

Section 4. Salaries and fees of state officers.

Except as provided in Arkansas Constitution, Article 19, Section 31, the General Assembly shall fix the salaries and fees of all officers in the State; and no greater salary or fee than that fixed by law shall be paid to any officer, employee, or other person, or at any rate other than par value; and the number and salaries of the clerks and employees of the different departments of the State shall be fixed by law.

Section 5. Property taxed according to value — Procedures for valuation — Tax exemptions.

(a) All real and tangible personal property subject to taxation shall be taxed according to its value, that value to be ascertained in such manner as the General Assembly shall direct, making the same equal and uniform throughout the State. No one species of property for which a tax may be collected shall be taxed higher than another species of property of equal value, except as provided and authorized in Section 15 of this Article, and except as authorized in Section 14 of this Article. The General Assembly, upon the approval thereof by a vote of not less than three-fourths (3/4ths) of the members elected to each house, may establish the methods and procedures for valuation of property for taxation purposes, but may not alter the method of valuation set forth in Section 15 of this Article. (b) The following property shall be exempt from taxation: public property used exclusively for public purposes; churches used as such; cemeteries used exclusively as such; school buildings and apparatus; libraries and grounds used exclusively for school purposes; and buildings and grounds and materials used exclusively for public charity. Nothing in this Section shall affect or repeal the provision of Amendment 57 to the Constitution of the State of Arkansas pertaining to intangible personal property.

Section 6. Other tax exemptions forbidden.

All laws exempting property from taxation, other than as provided in this Constitution shall be void.

Section 7. Taxation of corporate property.

The power to tax corporations and corporate property, shall not be surrendered or suspended by any contract or grant to which the State may be a party.

Section 8. Maximum rate of state taxes.

The General Assembly shall not have power to levy State taxes for any one year to exceed, in the aggregate, one per cent of the assessed valuation of the property of the State for that year.

Section 9. County taxes — Limitation.
No county shall levy a tax to exceed one-half of one per cent., for all purposes; but may levy an additional one-half of one per cent. to pay indebtedness existing at the time of the ratification of this Constitution.

Section 10. Payment of county and municipal taxes.
The taxes of counties, towns and cities shall only be payable in lawful currency of the United States, or the orders or warrants of said counties, towns and cities respectively.

Section 11. Levy and appropriation of taxes.
No tax shall be levied except in pursuance of law, and every law imposing a tax shall state distinctly the object of the same; and no moneys arising from a tax levied for any purpose shall be used for any other purpose.

Section 12. Disbursement of funds — Appropriation required.
Except as provided in Arkansas Constitution, Article 19, Section 31, no money shall be paid out of the treasury until the same shall have been appropriated by law; and then only in accordance with said appropriation.

Section 13. Illegal exactions.
Any citizen of any county, city or town may institute suit, in behalf of himself and all others interested, to protect the inhabitants thereof against the enforcement of any illegal exactions whatever.

Section 14. Procedure for adjustment of taxes after reappraisal or reassessment of property.
(a) Whenever a countywide reappraisal or reassessment of property subject to ad valorem taxes made in accordance with procedures established by the General Assembly shall result in an increase in the aggregate value of taxable real and personal property in any taxing unit in this State of ten percent (10%) or more over the previous year the rate of city or town, county,

school district, and community college district taxes levied against the taxable real and personal property of each such taxing unit shall, upon completion of such reappraisal or reassessment, be adjusted or rolled back, by the governing body of the taxing unit, for the year for which levied as provided below. The General Assembly shall, by law, establish the procedures to be followed by a county in making a countywide reappraisal or reassessment of property which will, upon completion, authorize the adjustment or rollback of property tax rates or millage, as authorized hereinabove. The adjustment or rollback of tax rates or millage for the "base year" as hereinafter defined shall be designed to assure that each taxing unit will receive an amount of tax revenue from each tax source no greater than ten percent (10%) above the revenues received during the previous year from each such tax source, adjusted for any lawful tax or millage rate increase or reduction imposed in the manner provided by law for the year for which the tax adjustment or rollback is to be made, and after making the following additional adjustments: (i) by excluding from such calculation the assessed value of, and taxes derived from, tangible personal property assessed in the taxing unit, and all real and tangible personal property of public utilities and regulated carriers assessed in the taxing unit, and (ii) by computing the adjusted or rollback millage rates on the basis of the reassessed taxable real property for the base year that will produce an amount of revenue no greater than ten percent (10%) above the revenues produced from the assessed value of real property in the taxing unit (after making the aforementioned adjustments for personal properties and properties of public utilities and regulated carriers noted above) from millage rates in effect in the taxing unit during the base year in which the millage adjustment or rollback is to be calculated. Provided, further, that in calculating the amount of adjusted or rollback millage necessary to produce tax revenues no greater than ten percent (10%) above the revenues received during the previous year, the governing body shall separate from the assessed value of taxable real property of the taxing unit, newly-discovered real property and new construction and improvements to real property, after making the adjustments for personal property or property of public utilities and regulated carriers noted above, and shall compute the millage necessary to produce an amount of revenues equal to, but no greater than the base year revenues of the taxing unit from each millage source. Such taxing unit may elect either to obtain an increase in revenues equal to the amount of revenues that the computed or adjusted rollback millage will produce from newly-discovered real property and new construction and improvements to real property, or if the same be less than ten percent (10%), the governing body of the taxing unit may recompute the millage rate to be charged to produce an amount no greater than ten percent (10%) above the revenues collected for taxable real property during the base year. Provided, however, that the amount of revenues to be derived from taxable personal property assessed in the taxing unit for the base year, other than personal property taxes to be paid by public utilities and regulated carriers in the manner provided hereinabove, shall be computed at the millage necessary to produce the same dollar amount of revenues derived during the current year in which the base year adjustment or rollback of millage is computed, and the millage necessary to produce the amount of revenues received from personal property taxes received by the taxing unit, for the base year shall be reduced annually as the assessed value of taxable personal property increases until the amount of revenues from personal property taxes, computed on the basis of the current year millage rates will produce an amount of revenues from taxable personal property equal to or greater than received during the base year, and thereafter the millage rates for computing personal property taxes shall be the millage rates levied for the current year. Provided, however, that the taxes to be paid by public utilities and regulated carriers in the respective taxing units of the several counties of this State during the first five (5) calendar years in which taxes are levied on the taxable real and personal property as reassessed and equalized in each of the respective counties as a part of a statewide reappraisal program, shall be the greater of the following: (1) the amount of taxes paid on property owned by such public utilities or regulated carriers in or assigned to such taxing unit, less adjustments for properties disposed of or reductions in the assessed valuation of such properties in the base year as defined below, or (2) the amount of taxes due on the assessed valuation of taxable real and tangible personal property belonging to the public utilities or regulated carriers located in or assigned to the taxing unit in each county at millage rates levied for the current year. As used herein, the term "base year" shall mean the year in which a county completes reassessment and equalization of taxable real and personal property as a part of a statewide reappraisal program, and extends the adjusted or rolled back millage rates for the first time, as provided in subsection (a) of this Section, for the respective taxing units in such county for collection in the following year. (i) in the event the amount of taxes paid the taxing unit in a county in the base year, as defined herein, is greater than the taxes due to be paid to such taxing unit for the current year of any year of the second (2nd) period of five (5) years after the base year, the difference between the base year taxes and the current year taxes for any year of such five (5) year period shall be adjusted as follows:

Current year of second period of (5) years
Taxes shall be current year taxes to which shall be added the following percentage of the difference between the current year taxes and the base year taxes (if greater than current year taxes) 1st year 80% of difference 2nd year 60% of difference 3rd year 40% of difference 4th year 20% of difference 5th year and thereafter Current years taxes only. (ii) If the current year taxes of a public utility or regulated carrier equal or exceed the base years taxes due a taxing unit during any year of the first ten (10) years after the base year, the amount of taxes to be paid to such taxing unit shall thereafter be the current years taxes and the adjustment authorized herein shall no longer apply in computing taxes to be paid to such taxing unit. Provided, that in the event the aforementioned requirement for payment of taxes by public utilities and regulated carriers, or any class of utilities or carriers for the ten (10) year period noted above, shall be held by court decision to be contrary to the constitution or statutes of this

State or of the Federal Government, the General Assembly may provide for other utilities or classes of carriers to receive the same treatment provided or required under the court order, if deemed necessary to promote equity between similar utilities or classes of carriers. (b) The General Assembly shall, by law, provide for procedures to be followed with respect to adjusting ad valorem taxes or millage pledged for bonded indebtedness purposes, to assure that the adjusted or rolled-back rate of tax or millage levied for bonded indebtedness purposes will, at all times, provide a level of income sufficient to meet the current requirements of all principal, interest, paying agent fees, reserves, and other requirements of the bond indenture.

Section 15. Assessment of residential property and agricultural, pasture, timber, residential and commercial land.
(a) Residential property used solely as the principal place of residence of the owner thereof shall be assessed in accordance with its value as a residence, so long as said property is used as the principal place of residence of the owner thereof, and shall not be assessed in accordance with some other method of valuation until said property ceases to be used for such residential purpose. (b) Agricultural land, pasture land, timber land, residential and commercial land, excluding structures thereon, used primarily as such, shall be valued for taxation purposes under the provisions of Section 5 of this Article, upon the basis of its agricultural, pasture, timber, residential, or commercial productivity or use, and when so valued, such land shall be assessed at the same percentum of value and taxed at the same rate as other property subject to ad valorem taxes. (c) The General Assembly shall enact laws providing for the administration and enforcement of this Section and for the imposition of penalties for violations of this Section, or statutes enacted pursuant thereto.

Section 16. Providing for exemption of value of residence of person 65 or over.

The General Assembly, upon approval thereof by a vote of not less than three-fourths (3/4ths) of the members elected to each house, may provide that the valuation of real property actually occupied by its owner as a residence who is sixty-five (65) years of age, or older, may be exempt in such amount as may be determined by law, but no greater than the first Twenty Thousand Dollars ($20,000) in value thereof, as a homestead from ad valorem property taxes.

Article XVII: Railroads, Canals and Turnpikes

Section 1. Common carriers — Construction of railroads.
All railroads, canals and turnpikes shall be public highways, and all railroads and canal companies shall be common carriers. Any association or corporation, organized for the purpose, shall have the right to construct and operate a railroad between any points within this State, and to connect at the State line with railroads of other States. Every railroad company shall have the right with its road to intersect, connect with, or cross any other road, and shall receive and transport each the other's passengers, tonnage and cars, loaded or empty, without delay or discrimination.

Section 2. Offices of common carriers.
Every railroad, canal or turnpike corporation operated, or partly operated in this State, shall maintain one office therein, where transfers of its stock shall be made and where its books shall be kept for inspection by any stockholder or creditor of such corporation; in which shall be recorded the amount of capital stock subscribed or paid in, and the amounts owned by them respectively, the transfer of said stock, and the names and places of residence of the officers.

Section 3. Equal right to transportation.
All individuals, associations and corporations shall have equal right to have persons and property transported over railroads, canals and turnpikes; and no undue or unreasonable discrimination shall be made in charges for, or in facilities for transportation of freight or passengers within the State, or coming from, or going to any other State. Persons and property transported over any railroad shall be delivered at any station at charges not exceeding the charges for transportation of persons and property of the same class, in the same direction, to any more distant station. But excursion and commutation tickets may be issued at special rates.

Section 4. Parallel or competing lines.

No railroad, canal or other corporation, or the lessees, purchasers or managers of any railroad, canal or corporation shall consolidate the stock, property or franchises of such corporation with, or lease, or purchase the works or franchises of, or in any way control any other railroad or canal corporation owning or having under its control a parallel or competing line, nor shall any officer of such railroad or canal corporation act as an officer of any other railroad or canal corporation owning or having control of a parallel or competing line; and the question whether railroads or canals are parallel or competing lines shall, when demanded by the party complainant, be decided by a jury as in other civil issues.

Section 5. Officers, agents and employees of carrier — Personal interest in contracts prohibited.

No president, director, officer, agent or employee of any railroad or canal company, shall be interested, directly or indirectly, in the furnishing of material or supplies to such company, or in the business of transportation as a common carrier of freight or passengers over the works owned, leased, controlled or worked by such company. Nor in any arrangement which shall afford more advantageous terms, or greater facilities than are offered or accorded to the public. And all contracts and arrangements in violation of this section shall be void.

Section 6. Discrimination by carriers.

No discrimination in charges, or facilities for transportation, shall be made between transportation companies and individuals, or in favor of either by abatement, drawback or otherwise; and no railroad or canal company, or any lessee, manager or employee thereof shall make any preferences in furnishing cars or motive power.

Section 7. Free passes.
The General Assembly shall prevent by law the granting of free passes by any railroad or transportation company to any officer of this State, legislative, executive or judicial.

Section 8. Condition of remission of forfeitures.
The General Assembly shall not remit the forfeiture of the charter of any corporation now existing, or alter or amend the same, or pass any general or special law for the benefit of such corporation, except on condition that such corporation shall thereafter hold its charter subject to the provisions of this Constitution.

Section 9. Right of eminent domain.
The exercise of the right of eminent domain shall never be abridged or so construed as to prevent the General Assembly from taking the property and franchises of incorporated companies, and subjecting them to public — use the same as the property of individuals.

Section 10. Regulation of carriers.
The General Assembly shall pass laws to correct abuses and prevent unjust discrimination and excessive charges by railroads, canals and turn-pike companies for transporting freight and passengers, and shall provide for enforcing such laws by adequate penalties and forfeitures, and shall provide for the creation of such offices and commissions and vest in them such authority as shall be necessary to carry into effect the powers hereby conferred.

Section 11. Movable property of carriers subject to execution.
That rolling stock and all other movable property belonging to any railroad company or corporation in this State shall be considered personal property, and shall be liable to execution and sale, in the same manner as the personal property of individuals, and the General Assembly shall pass no law exempting any such property from execution and sale.

Section 12. Damages by railroads to persons and property — Liability.
All railroads, which are now, or may be hereafter built, and operated either in whole or in part, in this State, shall be responsible for all damages to persons and property, under such regulations as may be prescribed by the General Assembly.

Section 13. Annual reports of railroads.
The directors of every railroad corporation shall annually make a report under oath to the Auditor of Public Accounts, of all of their acts and doings, which reports shall include such matters relating to railroads as may be prescribed by law, and the General Assembly shall pass laws enforcing, by suitable penalties, the provisions of this section.

Article XVIII: Judicial Circuits

Judicial Circuits

Until otherwise provided by the General Assembly, the Judicial Circuits shall be composed of the following counties: First — Phillips, Lee, St. Francis, Prairie, Woodruff, White and Monroe. Second — Mississippi, Crittenden, Cross, Poinsett, Craighead, Greene, Clayton and Randolph. Third — Jackson, Independence, Lawrence, Sharp, Fulton, Izard, Stone and Baxter. Fourth — Marion, Boone, Searcy, Newton, Madison, Carroll, Benton and Washington. Fifth — Pope, Johnson, Franklin, Crawford, Sebastian, Sarber and Yell. Sixth — Lonoke, Pulaski, Van Buren and Faulkner. Seventh — Grant, Hot Springs, Garland, Perry, Saline and Conway. Eighth — Scott, Montgomery, Polk, Howard, Sevier, Little River, Pike and Clark. Ninth — Hempstead, Lafayette, Nevada, Columbia, Union, Ouachita and Calhoun. Tenth — Chicot, Drew, Ashley, Bradley, Dorsey and Dallas. Eleventh — Desha, Arkansas, Lincoln and Jefferson.

Terms of Courts

Until otherwise provided by the General Assembly, the Circuit Courts shall be begun and held in the several counties as follows:

First Circuit

White — First Monday in February and August. Woodruff — Third Monday in February and August. Prairie — Second Monday after the third Monday in February and August. Monroe — Sixth Monday after the third Monday in February and August. St. Francis — Eighth Monday after the third Monday in February and August. Lee — Tenth Monday after the third Monday in February and August. Phillips — Twelfth Monday after the third Monday in February and August.

Second Circuit

Mississippi — First Monday in March and September. Crittenden — Second Monday in March and September. Cross — Second Monday after the second Monday in March and September. Poinsett — Third Monday after the second Monday in March and September. Craighead — Fourth Monday after the second Monday in March and September. Greene — Sixth Monday after the second Monday in March and September. Clayton — Seventh Monday after the second Monday in March and September. Randolph — Ninth Monday after the second Monday in March and September.

Third Circuit

Jackson — First Monday in March and September. Lawrence — Fourth Monday in March and September. Sharp — Second Monday after the fourth Monday in March and September. Fulton — Fourth Monday after the fourth Monday in March and September. Baxter — Sixth Monday after the fourth Monday in March and September. Izard — Seventh Monday after the fourth Monday in March and September. Stone — Ninth Monday after the fourth Monday in March and September. Independence — Tenth Monday after the fourth Monday in March and September.

Fourth Circuit

Marion — Second Monday in February and August. Boone — Third Monday in February and August. Searcy — Second Monday after the third Monday in February and August. Newton — Third Monday after the third Monday in February and August. Carroll — Fourth Monday after the third Monday in February and August. Madison — Fifth Monday after the third Monday in February and August. Benton — Sixth Monday after the third Monday in February and August. Washington — Eighth Monday after the third Monday in February and August.

Fifth Circuit

Greenwood District, Sebastian county — Third Monday in February and August. Fort Smith District, Sebastian county — First Monday after the fourth Monday in February and August. Crawford county — Fourth Monday after the fourth Monday in February and August. Franklin county — Sixth Monday after the fourth Monday in February and August. Sarber county — Eighth Monday after the fourth Monday in February and August. Yell county — Tenth Monday after the fourth Monday in February and August. Pope county — Twelfth Monday after fourth Monday in February and August. Johnson county — Fourteenth Monday after the fourth Monday in February and August.

Sixth Circuit

In the county of Pulaski on the first Monday in February, and continue twelve weeks if the business of said court require it. In the county of Lonoke on the first Monday succeeding the Pulaski Court, and continue two weeks if the business of said Court require it. In the county of Faulkner on the first Monday after the Lonoke Court, and continue two weeks if the business of said Court require it. In the county of Van Buren on the first Monday after the Faulkner Court, and continue two weeks if the business of said Court require it.

Fall Term, Sixth Circuit

In the county of Pulaski on the first Monday in October, and continue seven weeks if the business of said Court require it. In the county of Lonoke on the first Monday next after the Pulaski Court and continue two weeks if the business of said court require it. In the county of Faulkner on the first Monday after the Lonoke Court, and continue one week if the business of said Court require it. In the County of Van Buren on the first Monday after the Faulkner Court, and continue one week if the business of said Court require it.

Seventh Circuit

Hot Spring — Second Monday in March and September. Grant — Third Monday in March and September. Saline — Fourth Monday in March and September. Conway — Second Monday after fourth Monday in March and September. Perry — Fourth Monday after the fourth Monday in March and September. Garland — Fifth Monday after the fourth Monday in March and September.

Eighth Circuit

Montgomery — First Monday in February and August. Scott — First Monday after the first Monday in February and August. Polk — Second Monday after the first Monday in February and August. Sevier — Third Monday after the first Monday in February and August. Little River — Fifth Monday after the first Monday in February and August. Howard — Seventh Monday after the first Monday in February and August. Pike — Eighth Monday after the first Monday in February and August. Clark — Ninth Monday after the first Monday in February and August.

Ninth Circuit

Calhoun — First Monday in March and September. Union — Second Monday after the first Monday in March and September. Columbia — Fourth Monday after the first Monday in March and September. Lafayette—Sixth Monday after the first Monday in March and September. Hempstead — Eighth Monday after the first Monday in March and September. Nevada — Eleventh Monday after the first Monday in March and September. Ouachita — Thirteenth Monday after the first Monday in March and September.

Tenth Circuit

Dorsey — Third Monday in February and August. Dallas — First Monday in March and September. Bradley — Second Monday in March and September. Ashley — Third Monday in March and

September. Drew — Second Monday after the third Monday in March and September. Chicot — Fourth Monday after the third Monday in March and September.

Eleventh Circuit

In the county of Desha on the first Monday in March and September. In the county of Arkansas on the fourth Monday in March and September. In the county of Lincoln on the third Monday after the fourth Monday in March and September. In the county of Jefferson on the sixth Monday after the fourth Monday in March and September.

Article XIX: Miscellaneous Provisions

Section 1. Atheists disqualified from holding office or testifying as witness.
No person who denies the being of a God shall hold any office in the civil departments of this State, nor be competent to testify as a witness in any Court.

Section 2. Dueling.
No person who may hereafter fight a duel, assist in the same as second, or send, accept, or knowingly carry a challenge therefor, shall hold any office in the State, for a period of ten years; and may be otherwise punished as the law may prescribe.

Section 3. Elected or appointed officers — Qualifications of an elector required.
No persons shall be elected to, or appointed to fill a vacancy in, any office who does not possess the qualifications of an elector.

Section 4. Residence of officers.
All civil officers for the State at large shall reside within the State, and all district, county and township officers within their respective districts, counties and townships, and shall keep their offices at such places therein as are now, or may hereafter be required by law.

Section 5. Officers — Holding over.
All officers shall continue in office after the expiration of their official terms, until their successors are elected and qualified.

Section 6. Dual office holding prohibited.
No person shall hold or perform the duties of more than one office in the same department of the government at the same time, except as expressly directed or permitted by this Constitution.

Section 7. Residence — Temporary absence not to forfeit.

Absence on business of the State, or of the United States, or on a visit, or on necessary private business, shall not cause a forfeiture of residence once obtained.

Section 8. Deduction from salaries.

It shall be the duty of the General Assembly to regulate, by law in what cases, and what, deductions from the salaries of public officers shall be made for neglect of duty in their official capacity.

Section 9. Permanent state offices — Creation restricted.

The General Assembly shall have no power to create any permanent State Office, not expressly provided for by this Constitution.

Section 10. Election returns — State officers.

Returns for all elections, for officers who are to be commissioned by the Governor, and for members of the General Assembly, except as otherwise provided by this Constitution, shall be made to the Secretary of State.

Section 11.

Repealed.

Section 12. Receipts and expenditures to be published.

An accurate and detailed statement of the receipts and expenditures of the public money, the several amounts paid, to whom and on what account, shall, from time to time, be published as may be prescribed by law.

Section 13.

Repealed.

Section 14. Lotteries.
(a) The General Assembly may enact laws to establish, operate, and regulate State lotteries. (b) Lottery proceeds shall be used solely to pay the operating expenses of lotteries, including all prizes, and to fund or provide for scholarships and grants to citizens of this State enrolled in public and private non-profit two-year and four-year colleges and universities located within the State that are certified according to criteria established by the General Assembly. The General Assembly shall establish criteria to determine who is eligible to receive the scholarships and grants pursuant to this Amendment. (c) Lottery proceeds shall not be subject to appropriation by the General Assembly and are specifically declared to be cash funds held in trust separate and apart from the State treasury to be managed and maintained by the General Assembly or an agency or department of the State as determined by the General Assembly. (d) Lottery proceeds remaining after payment of operating expenses and prizes shall supplement, not supplant, non-lottery educational resources. (e) This Amendment does not repeal, supersede, amend or otherwise affect Amendment 84 to the Arkansas Constitution or games of bingo and raffles permitted therein. (f) Except as herein specifically provided, lotteries and the sale of lottery tickets are prohibited.

Section 15.

Repealed.

Section 16. Contracts for public buildings or bridges.
All contracts for erecting or repairing public buildings or bridges in any county, or for materials therefor; or for providing for the care and keeping of paupers, where there are no alms-houses, shall be given to the lowest responsible bidder, under such regulations as may be provided by law.

Section 17. Digest of laws — Publication.
The laws of this State, civil and criminal, shall be revised, digested, arranged, published and promulgated at such times and in such manner as the General Assembly may direct.

Section 18. Safety of miners and travelers.
The General Assembly, by suitable enactments, shall require such appliances and means to be provided and used as may be necessary to secure, as far as possible, the lives, health and safety of persons employed in mining, and of persons traveling upon railroads, and by other public conveyances, and shall provide for enforcing such enactments by adequate pains and penalties.

Section 19. Deaf and dumb and blind and insane persons.
It shall be the duty of the General Assembly to provide by law for the support of institutions for the education of the deaf and dumb, and of the blind; and also for the treatment of the insane.

Section 20. Oath of office.
Senators and Representatives, and all judicial and executive, State and county officers, and all other officers, both civil and military, before entering on the duties of their respective offices, shall take and subscribe to the following oath of affirmation: "I, _____ , do solemnly swear (or affirm) that I will support the Constitution of the United States and the Constitution of the State of Arkansas, and that I will faithfully discharge the duties of the office of _____ , upon which I am now about to enter."

Section 21. Sureties on official bonds — Qualifications — Bonding companies.
The sureties upon the official bonds of all State Officers shall be residents of, and have sufficient property within the State, not exempt from sale under execution, attachment or other process of any court, to make good their bonds and the sureties upon the official bonds of all county officers shall reside within the counties where such officers reside, and shall have sufficient

property therein, not exempt from such sale, to make good their bonds; provided, however, that any surety, bonding or guaranty company, organized for the purpose of doing a surety, or bonding business, and authorized to do business, in this State, may become surety on the bonds of all State, County and Municipal Officers under such regulations as may be prescribed by law.

Section 22. Constitutional amendments.
Either branch of the General Assembly, at a regular session thereof, may propose amendments to this Constitution; and if the same be agreed to by a majority of all members elected to each house, such proposed amendments shall be entered on the journals with the yeas and nays, and published in at least one newspaper in each county, where a newspaper is published, for six months immediately preceding the next general election for Senators and Representatives, at which time the same shall be submitted to the electors of the State, for approval or rejection; and if a majority of the electors voting at such election adopt such amendments, the same shall become a part of this Constitution. But no more than three amendments shall be proposed or submitted at the same time. They shall be so submitted as to enable the electors to vote on each amendment separately.

Section 23.

Repealed.

Section 24. Election contests.
The General Assembly shall provide by law the mode of contesting elections in cases not specifically provided for in this Constitution.

Section 25. Seal of state.

The present seal of the State shall be and remain the seal of the State of Arkansas until otherwise provided by law, and shall be kept and used as provided in this Constitution.

Section 26. Officers eligible to executive or judicial office.

Militia officers, and officers of the public schools, and Notaries may be elected to fill any executive or judicial office.

Section 27. Local improvements — Municipal assessments.

Nothing in this Constitution shall be so construed as to prohibit the General Assembly from authorizing assessments on real property for local improvements, in towns and cities, under such regulations as may be prescribed by law; to be based upon the consent of a majority in value of the property-holders owning property adjoining the locality to be affected; but such assessments shall be ad valorem and uniform.

Section 28. Contributions.

(a)(1) It is unlawful for a candidate for public office or a person acting on the candidates behalf to: (A) Accept a contribution from other than: (i) An individual; (ii) A political party that meets the definition of a political party under Arkansas Code Section 7-1-101; (iii) A political party that meets the requirements of Arkansas Code Section 7-7-205; (iv) A county political party committee; (v) A legislative caucus committee; or (vi) An approved political action committee; or (B) Accept a contribution in excess of the maximum amount allowed by law per election from: (i) An individual; (ii) A political party that meets the definition of a political party under Arkansas Code Section 7-1-101; (iii) A political party that meets the requirements of Arkansas Code Section 7-7-205; (iv) A county political party committee; (v) A legislative caucus committee; or (vi) An approved political action committee.
(2) A candidate may accept a contribution or contributions up to the maximum amount allowed by law from a prospective

contributor for each election, whether opposed or unopposed. (b)(1) It is unlawful for an individual, a political party that meets the definition of a political party under Arkansas Code Section 7-1-101, a political party that meets the requirements of Arkansas Code Section 7-7-205, a county political party committee, a legislative caucus committee, or an approved political action committee to make a contribution to a candidate for public office, or to a person acting on the candidate's behalf, that in the aggregate exceeds the maximum amount allowed by law. (2) The following entities may make a contribution or contributions up to the maximum amount allowed by law to a candidate, whether opposed or unopposed, for each election: (A) An individual; (B) A political party that meets the definition of a political party under Arkansas Code Section 7-1-101; (C) A political party that meets the requirements of Arkansas Code Section 7-7-205; (D) A county political party committee; (E) A legislative caucus committee; or (F) An approved political action committee. (c) As used in this section: (1)(A) "Approved political action committee" means any person that: (i) Receives contributions from one (1) or more persons in order to make contributions to a candidate, ballot question committee, legislative question committee, political party, county political party committee, or other political action committee; (ii) Does not accept any contribution or cumulative contributions in excess of five thousand dollars ($5,000) from any person in any calendar year; and (iii) Registers pursuant to Arkansas Code Section 7-6-215 prior to making contributions. (B) "Approved political action committee" does not include an organized political party as defined in Section 7-1-101, a county political party committee, the candidate's own campaign committee, an exploratory committee, or a ballot question committee or legislative question committee as defined in Section 7-9-402; (2) "Candidate" means an individual who has knowingly and willingly taken affirmative action, including solicitation of funds, for the purpose of seeking nomination for or election to any public office; (3)(A) "Contribution" or "contributions" means, whether direct or indirect, advances, deposits, or transfers of funds, contracts, or obligations, whether or not legally enforceable, payments, gifts, subscriptions, assessments, payment for services, dues, advancements, forbearance, loans, or pledges or promises of money or anything of value, whether or not legally enforceable, to a candidate, committee, or holder of elective office made for the purpose of influencing the nomination or election of any candidate.   (B)(i) "Contribution" or "contributions" includes the purchase of tickets for events such as dinners, luncheons, rallies, and similar fundraising events; the granting of discounts or rebates by television and radio stations and newspapers not extended on an equal basis to all candidates for the same office; and any payments for the services of any person serving as an agent of a candidate or committee by a person other than the candidate or committee or persons whose expenditures the candidates or committee must report under Arkansas law.   (ii) "Contribution" or "contributions" further includes any transfer of anything of value received by a committee from another committee.   (C) "Contribution" or "contributions" does not include noncompensated, nonreimbursed, volunteer personal services or travel;   (4) "County political party committee" means a person that: (A) Is organized at the county level for the purpose of supporting its affiliate party and making contributions;   (B) Is recognized by an organized political party, as defined in Arkansas Code Section 7-1-101, as being affiliated with that political party;   (C) Receives contributions from one (1) or more persons in order to make contributions to a candidate, ballot question committee, legislative question committee, political party, political action committee, or other county political party committee;   (D) Does not accept any contribution or cumulative contributions in excess of five thousand dollars ($5,000) from any person in any calendar year; and   (E) Registers pursuant to Arkansas Code Section 7-6-226 prior to making contributions;   (5)(A) "Election" means each election held to nominate or elect a candidate to any public office, including school elections.   (B) For the purposes of this section, a preferential primary, a general primary, a special election, and a general election shall each constitute a separate election;   (6) "Expenditure" or "expenditures" means a purchase, payment, distribution, gift, loan, or advance of money or anything of value, and a contract, promise, or agreement to make an expenditure, made for the purpose of influencing the nomination or election of any candidate;   (7)(A) "Exploratory committee" means a person that receives contributions which are held to be transferred to the campaign of a single candidate in an election.   (B) "Exploratory committee" does not include: (i) A political party: (a) That meets the definition of a political party under Arkansas Code Section 7-1-101; or   (b) A political party that meets the requirements of Arkansas Code Section 7-7-205; or (ii) The candidate's own campaign committee;   (8)(A) "Legislative caucus committee" means a person that is composed exclusively of members of the General Assembly, that elects or appoints officers and recognizes identified legislators as members of the organization, and that exists for research and other support of policy development and interests that the membership hold in common.   (B) "Legislative caucus committee" includes, but is not limited to, a political party caucus of the General Assembly, the Senate, or the House of Representatives.   (C) An organization whose only nonlegislator members are the Lieutenant Governor or the Governor is a legislative caucus committee for the purposes of this section;   (9)(A) "Person" means any individual, proprietorship, firm, partnership, joint venture, syndicate, labor union, business trust, company, corporation, association, committee, or any other organization or group of persons acting in concert.   (B) "Person" includes: (i) A political party that meets the definition of a political party under Arkansas Code Section 7-1-101 or a political party that meets the requirements of Arkansas Code Section 7-7-205;   (ii) A county political party committee; and   (iii) A legislative caucus committee; and   (10) "Public office" means an office created by or under authority of the laws of the State of Arkansas or of a subdivision thereof that is filled by the voters, except a federal office. (d)(1) A person who knowingly violates this section is guilty of a Class A misdemeanor.   (2) In addition to the penalty under subdivision (d)(1) of this section, the General Assembly shall provide by law for this section to be under the jurisdiction of the Arkansas Ethics Commission, including without limitation authorization of the following actions by the Arkansas Ethics Commission: (A) Promulgating reasonable rules to implement and administer this section as necessary;   (B) Issuing advisory opinions and guidelines on the requirements of this section; and   (C) Investigating complaints of alleged violations of this section and rendering findings and disciplinary action for such complaints. (e)(1) Except as provided in subdivision (e)(2) of this section, the General Assembly, in the same manner as required for amendment of laws initiated by the people, may amend this section so long as such amendments are germane to this section and consistent with its policy and purposes.   (2) The General Assembly may amend subsection (d) of this section by a majority vote of each house.

Section 29. Registration as a lobbyist by a former member of the General Assembly.

(a) A former member of the General Assembly shall not be eligible to be registered as a lobbyist under Arkansas Code Section 21-8-601 et seq. until two (2) years after the expiration of the term of office for which he or she was elected. (b) Subsection (a) of this section applies to all persons elected or reelected to the General Assembly on or after November 4, 2014. (c)(1) A person who knowingly violates this section is guilty of a Class D felony.   (2) In addition to the penalty under subdivision (c)(1) of this section, the General Assembly shall provide by law for this section to be under the jurisdiction of the Arkansas Ethics Commission, including without limitation authorization of the following actions by the Arkansas Ethics Commission: (A) Promulgating reasonable rules to implement and administer this section as necessary;   (B) Issuing advisory opinions and guidelines on the requirements of this section; and   (C) Investigating complaints of alleged violations of this section and rendering findings and disciplinary action for such complaints. (d)(1) Except as provided in subdivision (d)(2) of this section, the General Assembly, in the same manner as required for amendment of laws initiated by the people, may amend this section so long as such amendments are germane to this section and consistent with its policy and purposes. (2) The General Assembly may amend subsection (c) of this section by a majority vote of each house.

Section 30. Gifts from lobbyists.
(a) Persons elected or appointed to the following offices shall not knowingly or willfully solicit or accept a gift from a lobbyist, a person acting on behalf of a lobbyist, or a person employing or contracting with a lobbyist: (1) Governor; (2) Lieutenant Governor; (3) Secretary of State; (4) Treasurer of State (5) Auditor of State; (6) Attorney General; (7) Commissioner of State Lands; (8) Member of the General Assembly; (9) Chief Justice of the Supreme Court; (10) Justice of the Supreme Court; (11) Chief Judge of the Court of Appeals; (12) Judge of the Court of Appeals; (13) Circuit court judge; (14) District court judge; (15) Prosecuting attorney; and (16) Member of the independent citizens commission for the purpose of setting salaries of elected constitutional officers of the executive department, members of the General Assembly, justices, and judges under Article 19, Section 31, of this Constitution. (b) As used in this section: (1)(A) "Administrative action" means a decision on, or proposal, consideration, or making of a rule, regulation, ratemaking proceeding, or policy action by a governmental body. (B) "Administrative action" does not include ministerial action; (2)(A) "Gift" means any payment, entertainment, advance, services, or anything of value, unless consideration of equal or greater value has been given therefor. (B) "Gift" does not include: (i)(a) Informational material such as books, reports, pamphlets, calendars, or periodicals informing a person elected or appointed to an office under subsection (a) of this section regarding his or her official duties. (b) Payments for travel or reimbursement for any expenses are not informational material; (ii) Gifts that are not used and which, within thirty (30) days after receipt, are returned to the donor; (iii) Gifts from the spouse, child, parent, grandparent, grandchild, brother, sister, parent-in-law, brother-in-law, sister-in-law, nephew, niece, aunt, uncle, or first cousin of a person elected or appointed to an office under

subsection (a) of this section, or the spouse of any of these persons, unless the person is acting as an agent or intermediary for any person not covered by this subdivision (b)(2)(B)(iii); (iv) Anything of value that is readily available to the general public at no cost;   (v)(a)(1) Food or drink available at a planned activity to which a specific governmental body is invited, including without limitation a governmental body to which a person elected or appointed to an office under subsection (a) of this section is not a member.   (2) If a committee of the General Assembly is invited to a planned activity under subdivision (b)(2)(B)(v)(a)(1) of this section, only members of the committee of the General Assembly may accept food or drink at the planned activity.   (b)(1) As used in this subdivision (b)(2)(B)(v), "planned activity" means an event for which a written invitation is distributed electronically or by other means by the lobbyist, person acting on behalf of a lobbyist, or a person employing or contracting with a lobbyist to the members of the specific governmental body at least twenty-four (24) hours before the event.   (2) As used in this subdivision (b)(2)(B)(v), "planned activity" does not include food or drink available at a meeting of a specific governmental body for which the person elected or appointed to an office under subsection (a) of this section is entitled to receive per diem for attendance at the meeting.   (c) A lobbyist, a person acting on behalf of a lobbyist, or a person employing or contracting with a lobbyist shall not offer or pay for food or drink at more than one (1) planned activity in a seven-day period;   (vi)(a) Payments by regional or national organizations for travel to regional or national conferences at which the State of Arkansas is requested to be represented by a person or persons elected or appointed to an office under subsection (a) of this section.   (b) As used in this subdivision (b)(2)(B)(vi), "travel" means transportation, lodging, and conference registration fees.   (c) This section does not prohibit the acceptance of: (1) Food, drink, informational materials, or other items included in the conference registration fee; and   (2) Food and drink at events coordinated through the regional or national conference and provided to persons registered to attend the regional or national conference;

(vii) Campaign contributions;   (viii) Any devise or inheritance;   (ix) Salaries, benefits, services, fees, commissions, expenses, or anything of value in connection with: (a) The employment or occupation of a person elected or appointed to an office under subsection (a) of this section or his or her spouse so long as the salary, benefit, service, fee, commission, expense, or anything of value is solely connected with the person's employment or occupation and is unrelated to and does not arise from the duties or responsibilities of the office to which the person has been elected or appointed; or   (b) Service as an officer, director, or board member of a corporation, a firm registered to do business in the state, or other organization that files a state and federal tax return or is an affiliate of an organization that files a state and federal tax return by a person elected or appointed to an office under subsection (a) of this section or his or her spouse so long as the salary, benefit, service, fee, commission, expense, or anything of value is solely connected with the person's service as an officer, director, or board member and is unrelated to and does not arise from the duties or responsibilities of the office to which the person has been elected or appointed; and   (x) A personalized award, plaque, or trophy with a value of one hundred fifty dollars ($150) or less;   (3) "Governmental body" or "governmental bodies" means an office, department, commission, council, board, committee, legislative body, agency, or other establishment of the executive, judicial, or legislative branch of the state, municipality, county, school district, improvement district, or any political district or subdivision thereof;   (4)(A) "Income" means any money or anything of value received or to be received as a claim for future services, whether in the form of a retainer, fee, salary, expense, allowance, forbearance, forgiveness, interest, dividend, royalty, rent, or any other form of recompense or any combination thereof.   (B) "Income" includes a payment made under obligation for services or other value received;   (5) "Legislative action" means introduction, sponsorship, consideration, debate, amendment, passage, defeat, approval, veto, or any other official action or nonaction on any bill, ordinance, law, resolution, amendment, nomination, appointment, report, or other matter pending or proposed before a committee or house of the General Assembly, a quorum court, or a city council or board of directors of a municipality; (6) "Legislator" means a person who is a member of the General Assembly, a quorum court of a county, or the city council or board of directors of a municipality; (7) "Lobbying" means communicating directly or soliciting others to communicate with a public servant with the purpose of influencing legislative action or administrative action; (8) "Lobbyist" means a person who: (A) Receives income or reimbursement in a combined amount of four hundred dollars ($400) or more in a calendar quarter for lobbying one (1) or more governmental bodies; (B) Expends four hundred dollars ($400) or more in a calendar quarter for lobbying one (1) or more governmental bodies, excluding the cost of personal travel, lodging, meals, or dues; or (C) Expends four hundred dollars ($400) or more in a calendar quarter, including postage, for the express purpose of soliciting others to communicate with a public servant to influence any legislative action or administrative action of one (1) or more governmental bodies unless the communication has been filed with the Secretary of State or the communication has been published in the news media. If the communication is filed with the Secretary of State, the filing shall include the approximate number of recipients; (9)(A) "Person" means a business, individual, union, association, firm, committee, club, or other organization or group of persons. (B) As used in subdivision (b)(9)(A) of this section, "business" includes without limitation a corporation, partnership, sole proprietorship, firm, enterprise, franchise, association, organization, self-employed individual, receivership, trust, or any legal entity through which business is conducted; (10)(A) "Public appointee" means an individual who is appointed to a governmental body. (B) "Public appointee" does not include an individual appointed to an elective office; (11)(A) "Public employee" means an individual who is employed by a governmental body or who is appointed to serve a governmental body. (B) "Public employee" does not include a public official or a public appointee; (12) "Public official" means a legislator or any other person holding an elective office of any governmental body, whether elected or appointed to the office, and shall include such persons during the time period between the date they were elected and the date they took office; and (13) "Public servant" means all public officials, public employees, and public appointees. (c)(1) A person who knowingly violates this section is guilty of a Class B misdemeanor. (2) In addition to the penalty under subdivision (c)(1) of this section, the General Assembly shall provide by law for this section to be under the jurisdiction of the Arkansas Ethics Commission, including without limitation authorization of the following actions by the Arkansas Ethics Commission: (A) Promulgating reasonable rules to implement and administer this section as necessary;   (B) Issuing advisory opinions and guidelines on the requirements of this section; and   (C) Investigating complaints of alleged violations of this section and rendering findings and disciplinary action for such complaints. (3)(A) It is an affirmative defense to prosecution or disciplinary action under subdivisions (c)(1) and (2) of this section that a person elected or appointed to an office under subsection (a) of this section takes one (1) of the following actions within thirty (30) days of discovering or learning of an unintentional violation of this section: (i) Returns the gift to the donor; or   (ii) If the gift is not returnable, pays the donor consideration that is equal to or greater than the value of the gift.   (B)(i) The Arkansas Ethics Commission shall not proceed with an investigation of an alleged violation of this section if the Arkansas Ethics Commission determines that a person would be eligible to raise the affirmative defense under subdivision (c)(3)(A) of this section. (ii) If the Arkansas Ethics Commission does not proceed with an investigation of an alleged violation under subdivision (c)(3)(B)(i) of this section, the person shall not be considered to have committed a violation.   (C) This subdivision (c)(3) shall not be construed to authorize a person to knowingly or willfully solicit or accept a gift in violation of this section. (d)(1) Except as provided in subdivision (d)(2) of this section, the General Assembly, in the same manner as required for amendment of laws initiated by the people, may amend this section so long as such amendments are germane to this section and consistent with its policy and purposes. (2) The General Assembly may amend subsection (c) of this section by a majority vote of each house.

Section 31. Independent citizens commission.
(a) As provided in this section, members of the General Assembly shall have no authority to set salaries for: (1) Their positions as members of the General Assembly; (2) Elected constitutional officers of the executive department; (3) Justices; (4) Judges; and (5) Prosecuting attorneys. (b)(1) There is created an independent citizens commission for the purpose of setting salaries of elected constitutional officers of the executive department, members of the General Assembly, justices, judges, and prosecuting attorneys as provided in this section. (2)(A) Each member of the independent citizens commission shall serve a term of four (4) years. (B) A person shall not serve more than two (2) terms on the independent citizens commission. (3) The independent citizens commission shall consist of seven (7) members as follows: (A) Two (2) members appointed by the Governor; (B) Two (2) members appointed by the President Pro Tempore of the Senate; (C) Two (2) members appointed by the Speaker of the House of Representatives; and (D) One (1) member appointed by the Chief Justice of the Supreme Court. (4) Vacancies on the independent citizens commission shall be filled in the manner of the original appointment. (5) The independent citizens commission shall elect from its membership: (A) A chair; and (B) Other officers deemed necessary by the independent citizens commission. (6) Four (4) members of the independent citizens commission shall constitute a quorum for the purpose of transacting business. (7) A majority vote of the total membership of the independent citizens commission is required for any action of the independent citizens commission.
(8) The office of the Auditor of State shall provide staff assistance as may be requested by the independent citizens commission. (c)(1) In making appointments to the independent citizens commission, the Governor, the President Pro Tempore of the Senate, the Speaker of the House of Representatives, and

the Chief Justice of the Supreme Court shall consider racial, gender, and geographical diversity.   (2) A member of the independent citizens commission shall be: (A) A citizen of the United States;   (B) A resident of the State of Arkansas for at least two (2) years preceding his or her appointment;   (C) A qualified elector; and   (D) At least twenty-five (25) years of age.   (3) The following persons shall not serve on the independent citizens commission: (A) A person holding civil office;   (B) An employee of the State of Arkansas;   (C) A person required by law to register as a lobbyist; or   (D)(i) An immediate family member of: (a) A person holding civil office;   (b) An employee of the State of Arkansas; or   (c) A person required by law to register as a lobbyist.   (ii) As used in subdivision (c)(3)(D)(i) of this section, immediate family member means a person's spouse, a child of the person or spouse, a child's spouse, a parent of the person or the spouse, a brother or sister of the person or the spouse, anyone living or residing in the same residence or household with the person or the spouse, or anyone acting or serving as an agent of the person. (d) The independent citizens commission shall have the duty to review and adjust as it deems necessary the salaries for the following positions: (1) Governor;   (2) Lieutenant Governor;   (3) Attorney General;   (4) Secretary of State;   (5) Treasurer of State;   (6) Auditor of State;   (7) Commissioner of State Lands;   (8) Member of the General Assembly;   (9) Chief Justice of the Supreme Court;   (10) Justice of the Supreme Court;   (11) Chief Judge of the Court of Appeals;   (12) Judge of the Court of Appeals;   (13) Circuit court judge;   (14) District court judge; and   (15) Prosecuting attorney. (e)(1) The salaries of the positions under subsection (d) of this section: (A) Shall not be subject to appropriation by the General Assembly; and   (B) Shall be paid from the Constitutional Officers Fund or its successor fund or fund accounts in the amount determined by the independent citizens commission.   (2)(A) If the independent citizens commission proposes to adjust a salary for a position under subsection (d) of this section, the independent citizens commission shall: (i) Provide notice to the public of the proposed salary adjustment;   (ii) Make available to the public any data reviewed by the independent citizens commission in determining the proposed salary adjustment; and   (iii)(a) Afford the public a reasonable opportunity to provide public comment on the proposed salary adjustment.   (b) The opportunity for public comment under subdivision (e)(2)(A)(iii)(a) of this section shall not exceed forty-five (45) days.   (B) A proposed salary adjustment of the independent citizens commission shall not be considered a rule under the Arkansas Administrative Procedure Act, Arkansas Code Section 25-15-201 et seq.   (3) Upon satisfying (e)(2)(A)(i)-(iii) of this section, the independent citizens commission may file the adjusted salary with the Auditor of State.   (4) An adjustment to a salary shall be effective ten (10) days after it is filed with the Auditor of State.   (5) When considering whether or not to adjust a salary for a position under subsection (d) of this section, the independent citizens commission shall include in its considerations the overall economic condition of the state at that time. (f)(1)(A) The independent citizens commission, by a majority vote of the total membership of the independent citizens commission cast during its first regularly scheduled meeting of each calendar year, may authorize payment to its members of a stipend not to exceed eighty-five dollars ($85.00) per day for each meeting attended or for any day while performing any proper business of the independent citizens commission.   (B) Stipends shall be paid by the Auditor of State from funds available for that purpose.   (2) Members of the independent citizens commission shall receive no other compensation, expense reimbursement, or in-lieu-of payments. (g)(1) The independent citizens commission shall provide that the salaries of circuit judges be uniform throughout the state. (2)(A) Except as provided in this subdivision (g)(2), the independent citizens commission may increase or diminish the salaries for the positions under subsection (d) of this section. (B) The independent citizens commission may increase but not diminish the salaries for the positions under subdivisions (d)(9)-(14) of this section.   (3)(A) Except as provided in subdivision (g)(3)(B) and subdivision (m)(4)(B) of this section, no single adjustment at any one (1) time to a salary by the independent citizens commission shall exceed fifteen percent (15%) of the salary to be increased or diminished. (B) Salary adjustments resulting from the initial review of the independent citizens commission under subdivision (i)(3) of this section shall not be subject to subdivision (g)(3)(A) of this section. (4) The independent citizens commission shall provide for salaries to be paid in monthly installments. (h) Salaries for the positions under subsection (d) of this section shall continue as existing on November 4, 2014, until adjusted by the independent citizens commission. (i)(1) Initial members of the independent citizens commission shall be appointed within thirty (30) days of the effective date of this section. (2) The President Pro Tempore of the Senate shall call the first meeting of the independent citizens commission, which shall occur within forty-five (45) days of the effective date of this section. (3)(A) The independent citizens commission: (i) Shall complete an initial review of the salaries for the positions under subsection (d) of this section no later than ninety (90) days after the effective date of this section; and (ii) May file any adjustments in salary resulting from the initial review with the Auditor of State upon satisfying (e)(2)(A)(i)-(iii) of this section. (B) No later than ninety (90) days after the effective date of this section, the independent citizens commission shall also provide recommendations to the President Pro Tempore of the Senate and the Speaker of the House of Representatives concerning the amounts to be paid to members of the General Assembly for: (i) Per diem; (ii) Reimbursement for expenses; and (iii) Reimbursement for mileage. (4)(A) After completing the initial review under subdivision (i)(3) of this section, the independent citizens commission shall meet as necessary to review the salaries of the positions under subsection (d) of this section but shall not meet less than one (1) time per year. (B) The independent citizens commission may adjust the salaries of the positions under subsection (d) of this section as provided in this section as it deems necessary. (j) No later than ninety (90) days before the commencement of a regular session, the independent citizens commission shall provide recommendations to the President Pro Tempore of the Senate and the Speaker of the House of

Representatives concerning the amounts to be paid to members of the General Assembly for: (1) Per diem; (2) Reimbursement for expenses; and (3) Reimbursement for mileage. (k) The independent citizens commission shall be subject to the Freedom of Information Act of 1967, Arkansas Code Section 25-19-101 et seq. (l) The General Assembly, in the same manner as required for amendment of laws initiated by the people, may amend this section, so long as such amendments are germane to this section and consistent with its policy and purposes. (m)(1) Salaries for the positions under subdivision (d)(15) of this section shall continue as existing on November 4, 2014, until adjusted by the independent citizens commission. (2) No later than thirty (30) days after March 20, 2015, the independent citizens commission shall begin a study of salaries for the positions under subdivision (d)(15) of this section. (3) The independent citizens commission shall complete its review of the salaries for the positions under subdivision (d)(15) of this section no later than thirty (30) days after the date it begins its study under subdivision (m)(2) of this section. (4)(A) If at the conclusion of its study under subdivision (m)(2) of this section the independent citizens commission determines that a salary revision for the positions under subdivision (d)(15) is appropriate, the independent citizens commission shall propose an adjustment under subsection (e) of this section. (B) Initial salary revisions for the positions under subdivision (d)(15) resulting from the study under subdivision (m)(2) of this section are not subject to subdivision (g)(3)(A) of this section.

Article XX: "Holford" Bonds Not to Be Paid

The General Assembly shall have no power to levy any tax, or make any appropriations, to pay either the principal or interest, or any part thereof, of any of the following bonds of the State, or the claims, or pretended claims, upon which they may be based, to-wit: Bonds issued under an act of the General Assembly of the State of Arkansas, entitled, "An act to provide for the funding of the public debt of the State," approved April 6th, A. D. 1869, and numbered from four hundred and ninety-one to eighteen hundred and sixty, inclusive, being the "funding bonds," delivered to F. W. Caper, and sometimes called "Holford bonds;" or bonds known as railroad aid bonds, issued under an act of the General Assembly of the State of Arkansas, entitled, An act to aid in the construction of railroads, approved July 21, A. D. 1868; or bonds called "levee bonds," being bonds issued under an act of the General Assembly of the State of Arkansas, entitled "An act providing for the building and repairing the public levees of the State, and for other purposes," approved March 16, A. D. 1869, and the supplemental act thereto, approved April 12, 1869; and the act entitled "An act to amend an act entitled an act providing for the building and repairing of the public levees of this State," approved March 23, A. D. 1871, and any law providing for any such tax or appropriation, shall be null and void.

SCHEDULE

Section 1. Retention of existing laws — Sealed instruments.

All laws now in force, which are not in conflict or inconsistent with this Constitution, shall continue in force until amended or repealed by the General Assembly, and all laws exempting property from sale on execution, or by decree of a court, which were in force at the time of the adoption of the Constitution of 1868, shall remain in force with regard to contracts made before that time. Until otherwise provided by law no distinction shall exist between sealed and unsealed instruments, concerning contracts between individuals, executed since the adoption of the Constitution of 1868; Provided: That the statutes of limitation with regard to sealed and unsealed instruments in force at that time, continue to apply to all instruments afterward executed, and until altered or repealed.

Section 2.

Repealed.

Section 3. First general election.

An election shall be held at the several election precincts of every county in the State, on Tuesday, the thirteenth day of October, 1874, for Governor, Secretary of State, Auditor, Treasurer, Attorney-General, Commissioner of State Lands, (for two years unless the office is sooner abolished by the General Assembly), Chancellor, and Clerk of the separate Chancery court of Pulaski county, Chief Justice and two Associate Justices of the Supreme Court, a Circuit Judge and Prosecuting Attorney for each Judicial Circuit provided for in this Constitution; Senators and Representatives to the General Assembly, all county and township officers provided for in this Constitution; and also for the submission of this Constitution to the qualified electors of the State, for its adoption or rejection.

Section 4. Qualifications of voters.
The qualification of voters at the election, to be held as provided in this schedule, shall be the same as is now prescribed by law.

Section 5. Notice of election.
The State Board of Supervisors, hereinafter mentioned, shall give notice of said election immediately after the adoption of this Constitution by this Convention, by proclamation in at least two newspapers published at Little Rock, and such other newspapers as they may select. And each county board of Supervisors, shall give public notice in their respective counties, of said election, immediately after their appointment.

Section 6. Governor's proclamation.
The Governor shall also issue a proclamation enjoining upon all peace officers the duty of preserving good order on the day of said election, and preventing any disturbance of the same.

Section 7. State board of supervisors.
Augustus H. Garland, Gordon N. Peay and Dudley E. Jones are hereby constituted a State Board of Supervisors of said election, who shall take an oath faithfully and impartially to discharge the duties of their office; a majority of whom shall be a quorum, and who shall perform the duties herein assigned them. Should a vacancy occur in said Board, by refusal to serve, death, removal, resignation, or otherwise; or if any member should become incapacitated from performing said duties, the remaining members of the Board shall fill the vacancy by appointment. But if all the places on said Board become vacant at the same time, the said vacancies shall be filled by the President of this Convention.

Section 8. County board of supervisors.
Said State Board shall at once proceed to appoint a Board of Election Supervisors for each County of this State, consisting of three men of known intelligence and uprightness of character, who shall take the same oath as above provided for the State Board. A majority of each Board shall constitute a quorum, and

shall perform the duties herein assigned to them; and vacancies occurring in the County Boards shall be filled by the State Board.

Section 9. Poll books and ballot boxes — First election.
The State Board shall provide the form of poll books and each County Board shall furnish the Judges of each election precinct with three copies of the poll books in the form prescribed, and with ballot-boxes at the expense of the county.

Section 10. Copies of Constitution to be distributed.
The State Board of Supervisors shall cause to be furnished in pamphlet form a sufficient number of copies of this Constitution to supply each County Supervisor and Judge of Election with a copy, and shall forward the same to the County Election Boards for distribution.

Section 11. Judges and clerks of first election.
The Boards of County Election Supervisors shall at once proceed to appoint three Judges of Election for each election precinct in their respective counties; and the Judges shall appoint three Election Clerks for their respective precincts, all of whom shall be good, competent men, and take an oath as prescribed above. Should the Judges of any election precinct fail to attend at the time and place provided by law, or decline to act, the assembled electors shall choose competent persons, in the manner provided by law, to act in their place, who shall be sworn as above.

Section 12. Conduct of first election.
Said election shall be conducted in accordance with existing laws, except as herein provided. As the electors present themselves at the polls to vote, the judges of the election shall pass upon their qualifications and the clerks of the election shall register their names on the poll-books if qualified; and such registration by said clerks shall be a sufficient registration in conformity with the Constitution of this State, and then their votes shall be taken.

Section 13. Style of ballot.
Each elector shall have written or printed on his ticket "For Constitution," or "Against Constitution," and also the offices and the names of the candidates for the offices for whom he desires to vote.

Section 14. Manner of voting.
The judges shall deposit the tickets in the ballot-box; but no elector shall vote outside of the township or ward in which he resides. The names of the electors shall be numbered, and the corresponding numbers shall be placed on the ballots by the judges when deposited.

Section 15. Dram shops to be closed — First election.
All dram shops and drinking houses in this State shall be closed during the day of said election, and the succeeding night; and any person selling or giving away intoxicating liquors during said day or night shall be punished by fine, not less than two hundred dollars, for each and every offense, or imprisoned not less than six months, or both.

Section 16. Hours of voting — Counting of ballots — Returns.
The polls shall be opened at eight o'clock in the forenoon, and shall be kept open until sunset. After the polls are closed the ballots shall be counted by the judges at the place of voting, as soon as the polls are closed, unless prevented by violence or accident; and the results by them certified on the poll-books, and the ballots sealed up. They shall be returned to the County Board of Election Supervisors, who shall proceed to cast up the votes and ascertain and state the number of votes cast for the Constitution and the number cast against the Constitution, and also the number of votes cast for each candidate voted for for any office, and shall forthwith forward to the State Board of Supervisors, duly certified by them, one copy of the statement or abstracts of the votes so made out by them, retain one copy in their possession, and file one copy in the office of the County Clerk, where they shall also deposit, for safe-keeping, the ballots,

sealed up, and one copy of the poll-books, retaining possession of the other copies.

Section 17. Publication of result.
The State Board of Supervisors shall at once proceed, on receiving such returns from the County Boards, to ascertain therefrom, and state the whole number of votes given for the Constitution, and the whole number given against it; and if a majority of all votes cast in favor of the Constitution, they shall at once make public the fact by publication in two or more of the leading newspapers published in the city of Little Rock, and this Constitution, from that date, shall be in force; and they shall also make out and file, in the office of the Secretary of State an abstract of all the votes cast for the Constitution, and all votes cast against it; and also an abstract of all votes cast for every candidate voted for at the election, and file the same in the office of the Secretary of State, showing the candidate elected. They shall also make out and certify, and lay before each house of the General Assembly a list of the members elected to that house; and shall also make out, certify and deliver to the Speaker of the House of Representatives an abstract of all votes cast at the election, for any and all persons for the office of Governor, Secretary of State, Treasurer of State, Auditor of State, Attorney General and Commissioner of State Lands, and the said Speaker shall cast up the votes and announce the names of the persons elected to these offices. The Governor, Secretary of State, Treasurer of State, Auditor of State, Attorney-General and Commissioner of State Lands chosen at said election shall qualify and enter upon the discharge of the duties of their respective offices within fifteen days after the announcement of their election as aforesaid.

Section 18. Commissions — Officers elected at first election.
All officers shown to be elected by the abstract of said election filed by the State Board of Supervisors in the office of the Secretary of State, required by this Constitution to be commissioned, shall be commissioned by the Governor.

Section 19. Election of representatives and senators — First election.

At said election the qualified voters of each County and Senatorial District, as defined in article eight of this Constitution, shall elect, respectively, Representatives and Senators according to the numbers and apportionment contained in said article. The Board of Election Supervisors of each county shall furnish certificates of election to the person or persons elected to the House of Representatives as soon as practicable after the result of the election has been ascertained; and such Board of Election Supervisors in each county shall make a correct return of the election for Senator or Senators to the Board of Election Supervisors of the county first named in the Senatorial apportionment, and said Board shall furnish certificates of election to the person or persons elected as Senator or Senators in said Senatorial district as soon as practicable.

Section 20. When officers to enter upon duties.

All officers elected under this Constitution, except the Governor, Secretary of State, Auditor of State, Treasurer, Attorney-General and Commissioner of State Lands shall enter upon the duties of their several offices when they shall have been declared duly elected by said State Board of Supervisors, and shall have duly qualified. All such officers shall qualify and enter upon the duties of their offices within fifteen days after they have been duly notified of their election.

Section 21. Prior incumbents to vacate office.

Upon the qualification of the officers elected at said election the present incumbents of the offices for which the election is held shall vacate the same and turn over to the officers thus elected and qualified, all books, papers, records, moneys and documents belonging or pertaining to said offices by them respectively held.

Section 22. First session of General Assembly.

The first session of the General Assembly under this constitution shall commence on the first Tuesday after the second Monday in November, 1874.

Section 23. Transfer of jurisdiction of courts.
The County Courts provided for in this Constitution shall be regarded in law as a continuation of the Boards of Supervisors now existing by law, and the Circuit Courts shall be regarded in law as continuations of the Criminal Courts wherever the same may have existed in their respective counties: and the Probate Courts shall be regarded as continuations of the Circuit Courts for the business within the jurisdiction of such Probate Courts, and the papers and records pertaining to said courts and jurisdictions shall be transferred accordingly; and no suit or prosecution of any kind shall abate because of any change made in this Constitution.

Section 24. Present incumbents to hold until successors qualify.
All officers now in office whose offices are not abolished by this Convention, shall continue in office and discharge the duties imposed on them by law, until their successors are elected and qualified under this Constitution. The office of Commissioner of State Lands shall be continued; Provided, That the General Assembly at its next session may abolish or continue the same in such manner as may be prescribed by law.

Section 25. Fraud in first election.
Any election officer, appointed under the provisions of this schedule, who shall fraudulently and corruptly permit any person to vote illegally or refuse the vote of any qualified elector, cast up or make a false return of said election, shall be deemed guilty of a felony, and on conviction thereof, shall be imprisoned in the penitentiary not less than five years nor more than ten years. And any person who shall vote when not a qualified elector, or vote more than once, or bribe any one to vote contrary to his wishes, or intimidate or prevent any elector by threats, menace or promises from voting, shall be guilty of a felony, and upon conviction thereof, shall be imprisoned in the penitentiary not less than one, nor more than five years.

Section 26. Tenure of officers elected.

All officers elected at the election provided for in this schedule shall hold their offices for the respective periods provided for in the foregoing Constitution, and until their successors are elected and qualified. The first general elections after the ratification of this Constitution shall be held on the first Monday of September A. D. 1876. Nothing in this Constitution and the schedule thereto shall be so construed as to prevent the election of congressmen at the time as now prescribed by law.

Section 27. Appropriation for expenses of election.

The sum of five thousand dollars is hereby appropriated out of any money in the treasury, not otherwise appropriated, to defray the expenses of the election provided for in this schedule, and the Auditor of State shall draw his warrants on the Treasurer for such expenses, not exceeding said amount, on the certificate of the State Board of Supervisors of election.

Section 28. Salaries of officers.

For the period of two years from the adoption of this Constitution, and until otherwise provided by law, the respective officers herein enumerated shall receive for their services the following salaries per annum:

For Governor, the sum of $3,500

For Secretary of State, the sum of 2,000

For Treasurer, the sum of 2,500

For Auditor, the sum of 2,500

For Attorney General, the sum of 2,000

For Commissioner of State Lands, the sum of 2,000

For Judges of Supreme Court, each, the sum of 3,500

For Judges of Circuit and Chancery Courts, each, the sum of 2,500

For Prosecuting Attorneys, each, the sum of 400

For members of the General Assembly, the sum of $6 per day, and twenty cents per mile for each mile traveled in going to and returning from the seat of government over the most direct and practicable route.

Done in Convention, at Little Rock, the Seventh day of September in the year of our Lord one thousand eight hundred and seventy four and of the Independence of the United States the ninety-ninth.

In Witness Whereof, we have hereunto subscribed our names. GRANDISON D. ROYSTON, President of the Convention, and Delegate from the County of Hempstead. THOMAS W. NEWTON, Secretary.

A. M. RODGERS, Delegate from Benton County.
HORACE H. PATTERSON, Delegate from Benton County.
W. W. BAILEY, Delegate from Boone County.
JNO. R. HAMPTON, Delegate from Bradley County.
JOHN W. CYPERT, Delegate from Baxter County.
BRADLEY BUNCH, Delegate from Carroll County.
JESSE A. ROSS, Delegate from Clark County.
H. F. THOMASON, Delegate from Crawford County.
W. D. LEIPER, Delegate from Dallas County.
WM. J. THOMPSON, Delegate from Woodruff County.
JAMES A. GIBSON, Delegate from Arkansas County.
HENRY W. CARTER, Delegate from Pike County.
DANIEL F. REINHARDT, Delegate from Prairie County.
ELIJAH MOSELEY, Delegate from Ouachita County.
STEPHEN C. BATES, Delegate from Polk County.
G. P. SMOOTE, Delegate from Columbia County.
D. L. KILLGORE, Delegate from Columbia County.
WILLIAM S. HANNA, Delegate from Conway County.

JOHN S. ANDERSON, Delegate from Craighead County.
J. G. FRIERSON, Delegate from Cross County.
E. FOSTER BROWN, Delegate from Clayton County.
JAS. P. STANLEY, Delegate from Drew County.
JOHN NIVEN, Delegate from Dorsey County.
WILLIAM W. MANSFIELD, Delegate from the County of Franklin.
JOHN DUNAWAY, Delegate from the County of Faulkner.
DAVIDSON D. CUNNINGHAM, Delegate from the County of Grant.
BEN H. CROWLEY, Delegate from the County of Greene.
H. M. RECTOR, Delegate from Garland County.
JN. R. EAKIN, Delegate from Hempstead County.
W. C. KELLY, Delegate from Hot Spring County.
J. W. BUTLER, Delegate from Independence County.
JAMES RUTHERFORD, Delegate from Independence County.
RANSOM GULLEY, Delegate from Izard County.
FRANKLIN DOSWELL, Delegate from Jackson County.
JNO. A. WILLIAMS, Delegate from Jefferson County.
SETH J. HOWELL, Delegate from Johnson County.
PHILIP K. LESTER, Delegate from Lawrence County.
J. H. WILLIAMS, Delegate from Little River County.
J. P. EAGLE, Delegate from Lonoke County.
REASON G. PUNTNEY, Delegate from Lincoln County.
MONROE ANDERSON, Delegate from Lee County.
JOHN CARROLL, Delegate from Madison County.
S. P. HUGHES, Delegate from Monroe County.
NICHOLAS W. CABLE, Delegate from Montgomery County.
CHARLES BOWEN, Delegate from Mississippi County.
R. K. GARLAND, Delegate from Nevada County.
HENRY G. BUNN, Delegate from Ouachita County.
W. H. BLACKWELL, Delegate from Perry County.
JNO. J. HORNOR, Delegate from Phillips County.
JNO. R. HOMER SCOTT, Delegate from the County of Pope.
JOHN MILLER, JR., Delegate from the County of Randolph.
SIDNEY M. BARNES, Delegate from the County of Pulaski.
JABEZ M. SMITH, Delegate from Saline County.
BEN B. CHISM, Delegate from the County of Sarber.
J. W. SORRELS, Delegate from Scott County.

W. S. LINDSEY, Delegate from Searcy County.
R. P. PULLIAM, Delegate from Sebastian County.
W. M. FISHBACK, Delegate from Sebastian County.
B. H. KINSWORTHY, Delegate from Sevier County.
LEWIS WILLIAMS, Delegate from Sharp County.
JOHN M. PARROTT, Delegate from Saint Francis County.
WALTER J. CAGLE, Delegate from Stone County.
HORATIO G. P. WILLIAMS, Delegate from Union County.
ROBT. GOODWIN, Delegate from Union County.
A. R. WITT, Delegate from Van Buren County.
R. P. POLK, Delegate from Phillips County.
T. W. THOMASON, Delegate from Washington County.
BENJAMIN F. WALKER, Delegate from Washington County.
M. F. LAKE, Delegate from Washington County.
JESSE N. CYPERT, Delegate from White County.
J. W. HOUSE, Delegate from White County.
JOSEPH T. HARRISON, Delegate from Yell County.
MARCUS L. HAWKINS, Delegate from Ashley County.
EDWIN R. LUCAS, Delegate from Fulton County.
BENJAMIN W. JOHNSON, Delegate from Calhoun County.
RODERICK JOYNER, Delegate from Poinsett County.

PROCLAMATION
By The STATE BOARD OF ELECTION SUPERVISORS

Office of State Board of Election Supervisors, Little Rock, Ark., October 30, 1874.

In pursuance of the provisions of section seventeen of the schedule to the Constitution recently framed for the State of Arkansas, the undersigned do hereby proclaim and make known that at a general election held on the thirteenth day of October, A. D. 1874, the following votes were cast "For" and "Against" said Constitution in the several counties of said State, as appears by the official returns made to said board by the county boards of election supervisors, to-wit:

Here follows a tabulation of the vote by counties.

Total Vote "For Constitution" 78,697

Total Vote "Against Constitution" 24,807

Majority "For Constitution" 53,890

Given under our hands this thirtieth day of October, 1874.

U. M. ROSE, DUDLEY E. JONES, GORDON N. PEAY, State Board of Election Supervisors.